…they walked beside the ocean
of the end and the beginning.

—George Mackay Brown

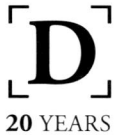

D
20 YEARS

Cofounders: Taj Forer and Michael Itkoff
Creative Director: Ursula Damm
Copy Editor: Gabrielle Fastman

ISBN: 978-1-9541192-4-6

Printed by Ofset Yapimevi, Turkey

Daylight Books
E-mail: info@daylightbooks.org
Web: www.daylightbooks.org

Alicia Bruce

I BURN BUT I AM NOT CONSUMED

Daylight

Birds migrate over
a once-mobile dune
system which has been
stabilised by marram
grass allegedly planted
by local schoolchildren
invited by Trump
International Golf Links
Scotland to a nature
workshop in 2009;
March 2011.

4

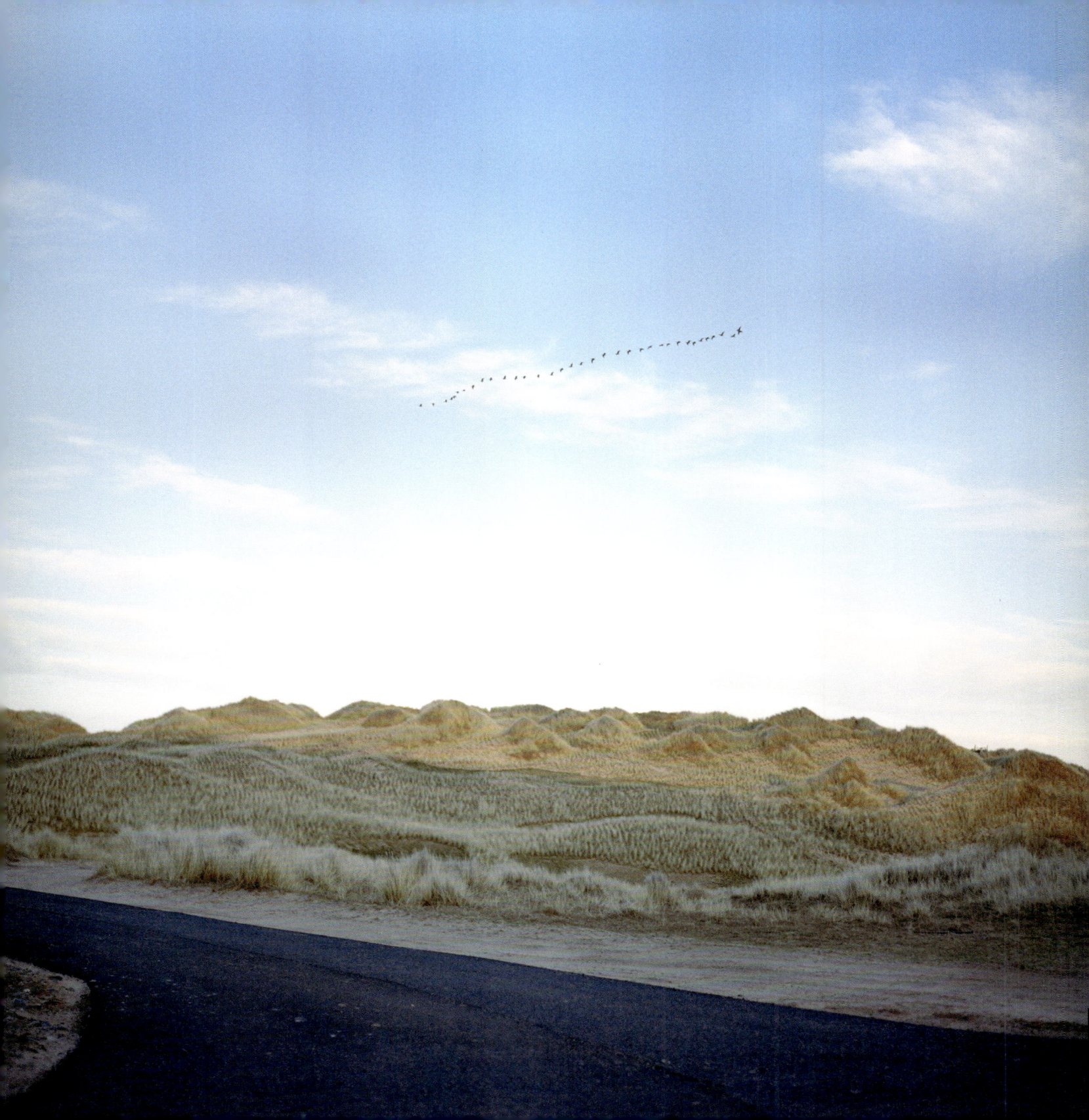

FOREWORD

by Alicia Bruce

"His property is terribly maintained. It's slum-like. It's disgusting. He's got stuff thrown all over the place. He lives like a pig."[1]

This is how Mike Forbes, a Scottish crofter and quarryman, was described by Donald Trump in 2006. At the time, Trump was an American developer who jetted into Aberdeenshire with claims that he would build 'the greatest golf course in the world'[2] on a Site of Special Scientific Interest (a conservation designation for protected land) and dynamic dune system on the north-east coast of Scotland. Mike reflected on his response at the time in a recent conversation we had: "I said, if I'm the village idiot, he must be the New York clown, which proved to be true! If he came back to ma door, I would smack him one. That's what I should have done when I first met him. I should have knocked him on his arse then."[3] Their story was compared to David and Goliath in the press, and as someone who grew up in the area, I couldn't quite believe all I was reading. This was several years before Trump would become the US president and declare any negative reports about himself 'fake news'.

This book honours a Scottish coastal community who refused to bow down, sell up, or be pushed around by Donald Trump. It is a document of a remarkable people; they stood up to money, power, and bullying to save their once-protected land

1 *Late Show with David Letterman*, 2006.
2 *Late Show with David Letterman*, 2006.
3 Mike Forbes audio interview with Alicia Bruce, Mill of Menie, 9 July 2022.

and homes from compulsory purchase, a process by which a public authority has the power to take private land for projects deemed in the public interest.

Donald Trump announced his plans to build his golf complex and housing development in Menie, near Balmedie beach, in 2006. I had fond childhood memories of playing on Balmedie's huge sand dunes, and I was saddened to see this happening. Red carpets were being rolled out for the American businessmen and the local press were vocally in favour. I followed with interest and shock as local councillors who rejected Trump's plans were labelled 'traitors' and 'neeps' in the local press, with their faces photoshopped onto neeps, the word for turnips in Doric, the local dialect. But residents portrayed as 'opponents' and 'peasants' were eventually recognised as local heroes and national treasures.

The fanfare around Trump at this time was astounding; Aberdeen's Robert Gordon University awarded him an honorary doctorate in October 2010. By 2015, he had been stripped of this title due to racist comments he'd made.

As a photographer, my role in Menie is to be a conduit for my friends there. They have lived in the shadow of Trump, and with the impact of his plans for their homes and land, for too long. Through my collaborations with the Menie residents, I have learned that even as a working-class photographer without money or power, I can assist others in sharing their worldviews and personal stories in alternative ways. I try to help, in my own way, make social change for the better. A book is more accessible to many than an exhibition or an archive, and it is my intention that this book preserves this important story within the wider context of Scottish history. I hope that this collection will survive as a lasting record of the land and residents of Menie, remembering especially my friends Molly Forbes, Sheila Forbes, and Susan Munro, whom we lost during the Covid-19 pandemic, and Mickey Foote, who passed away in 2018. I've witnessed firsthand the impact this development has had on a community that, when all is said and done, just wanted to be left in peace. They became reluctant celebrities, thrust against their will into the media spotlight to save their homes and protect the landscape that they knew and loved.

Several of the portraits in this book were made in reference to existing oil paintings. Traditionally, you would visit a gallery to see what's crassly named 'the great and the good' on the walls, and I wanted to give that same weight, attention, and symbolism to the residents of Menie; not to monumentalise, but to secure their story in our cultural imagination.

My wish is that others will see through this lens the importance of integrity, compassion, and stewardship of our natural world above profit, power, and TV personalities.

It was when the proposals came in to sacrifice the Site of Special Scientific Interest (SSSI) that the whole thing really kicked off for me. That was when I took a better look at what was meant to be the trade-off and found there wasn't one. After all, the SSSI is a supposedly protected site meant to be retained to help keep the balance of the planet, and here it was, being sacrificed for some unprovable economic benefit. When we looked more closely it became obvious, even, that it was all down to a very qualified appraisal that has never yet been looked at by any independent organisation.

This was long before there was any threat against our homes. It was in March 2009 that lawyers for T3 [Trump] applied for compulsory purchase over our homes and October that year that Aberdeenshire Council failed to make a decision on this subject. We have now endured two Christmases with this threat hanging over us, all five households, and our position has not changed, and no substantive contact has been made by T3.

The SSSI has been dug away and no one knows what effect this will have on Forvie nature reserve further north or the wildlife that used to live in this area. The reputation of the North East of Scotland has been irreparably damaged by the cavalier and cowardly actions of a small group of politicians and self-interested businesspeople who seem to think they can do no wrong, and that the long-term environmental destruction caused by this housing development is acceptable, as long as they make a profit. They are wrong.

It needs to be remembered by all that we do not inherit this earth from our ancestors; we borrow it from our descendants.

—David Milne, Menie resident, 2010

I'm going to call it 'The Great Dunes of Scotland'.

—Donald Trump, Aberdeenshire, 2006

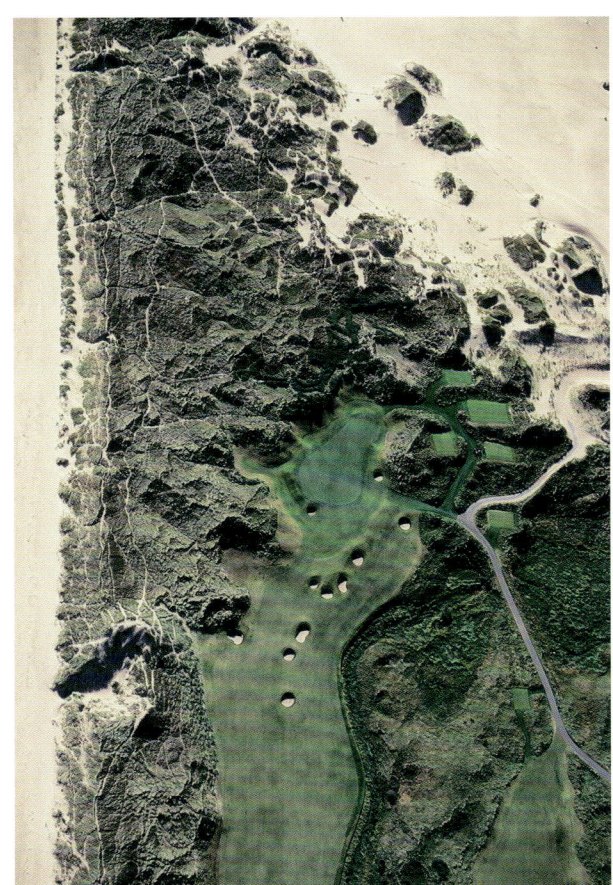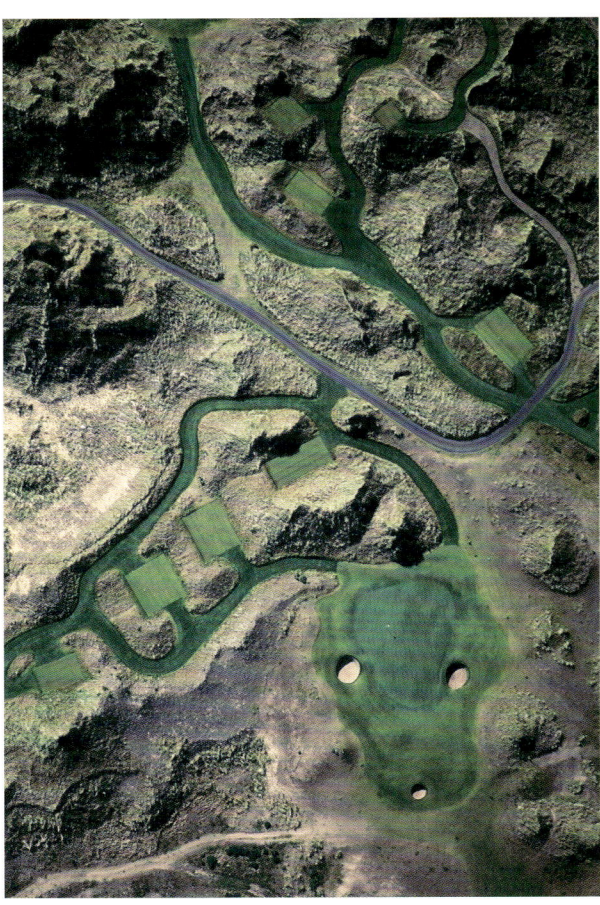

Above: From the *Playgrounds* series: bunkered terrain, Menie, and Trump International Golf Links on the remains of the dunes at Menie, 2015. (Reproduced with kind permission from Patricia and Angus Macdonald.)

Right: The original Trump International Golf Links Scotland developers' map, designed by golf architects Hawtree Ltd. These original designs relied on a Compulsory Purchase Order (CPO) of Menie residents' homes. The resort hotel and holiday homes were never built. The area shaped like a cross marked 'NOT A PART' is Mill of Menie, property of Mike Forbes. Leyton Cottage, the home of the Munros, and Hermit Point, home of the Milnes, are also labelled. The first golf course opened 10 July 2012 with a temporary clubhouse.

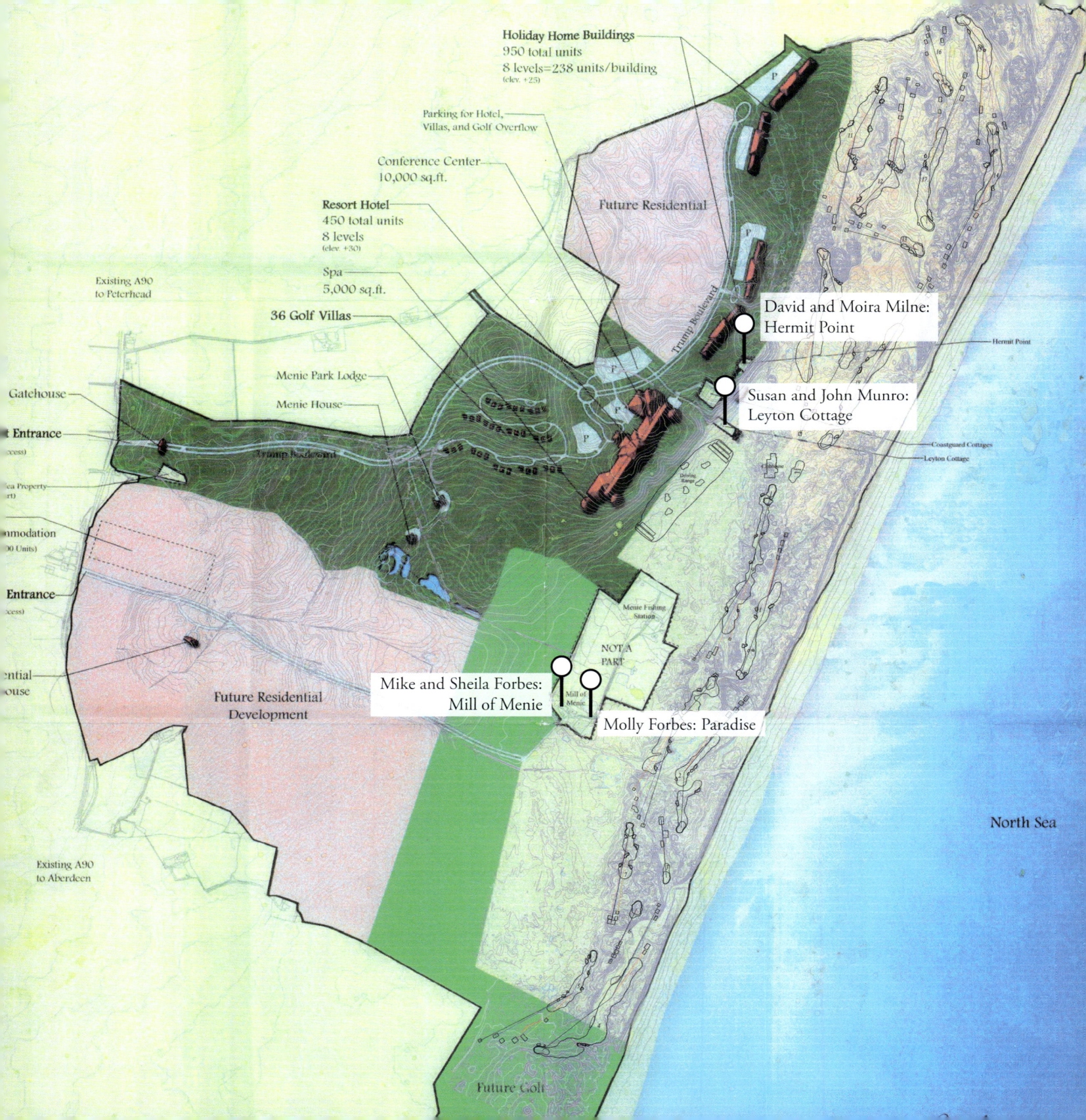

Holiday Home Buildings
950 total units
8 levels=238 units/building
(elev. +25)

Parking for Hotel,
Villas, and Golf Overflow

Conference Center
10,000 sq.ft.

Resort Hotel
450 total units
8 levels
(elev. +30)

Spa
5,000 sq.ft.

36 Golf Villas

Future Residential

David and Moira Milne:
Hermit Point

Hermit Point

Susan and John Munro:
Leyton Cottage

Coastguard Cottages

Leyton Cottage

Existing A90
to Peterhead

Gatehouse

Entrance
(ccess)

ea Property
(art)

Menie Park Lodge

Menie House

Trump Boulevard

mmodation
00 Units)

Entrance
(ccess)

ential
ouse

Future Residential
Development

Menie Fishing
Station

NOT A
PART

Mill of
Menie

Mike and Sheila Forbes:
Mill of Menie

Molly Forbes: Paradise

North Sea

Existing A90
to Aberdeen

Future Golf

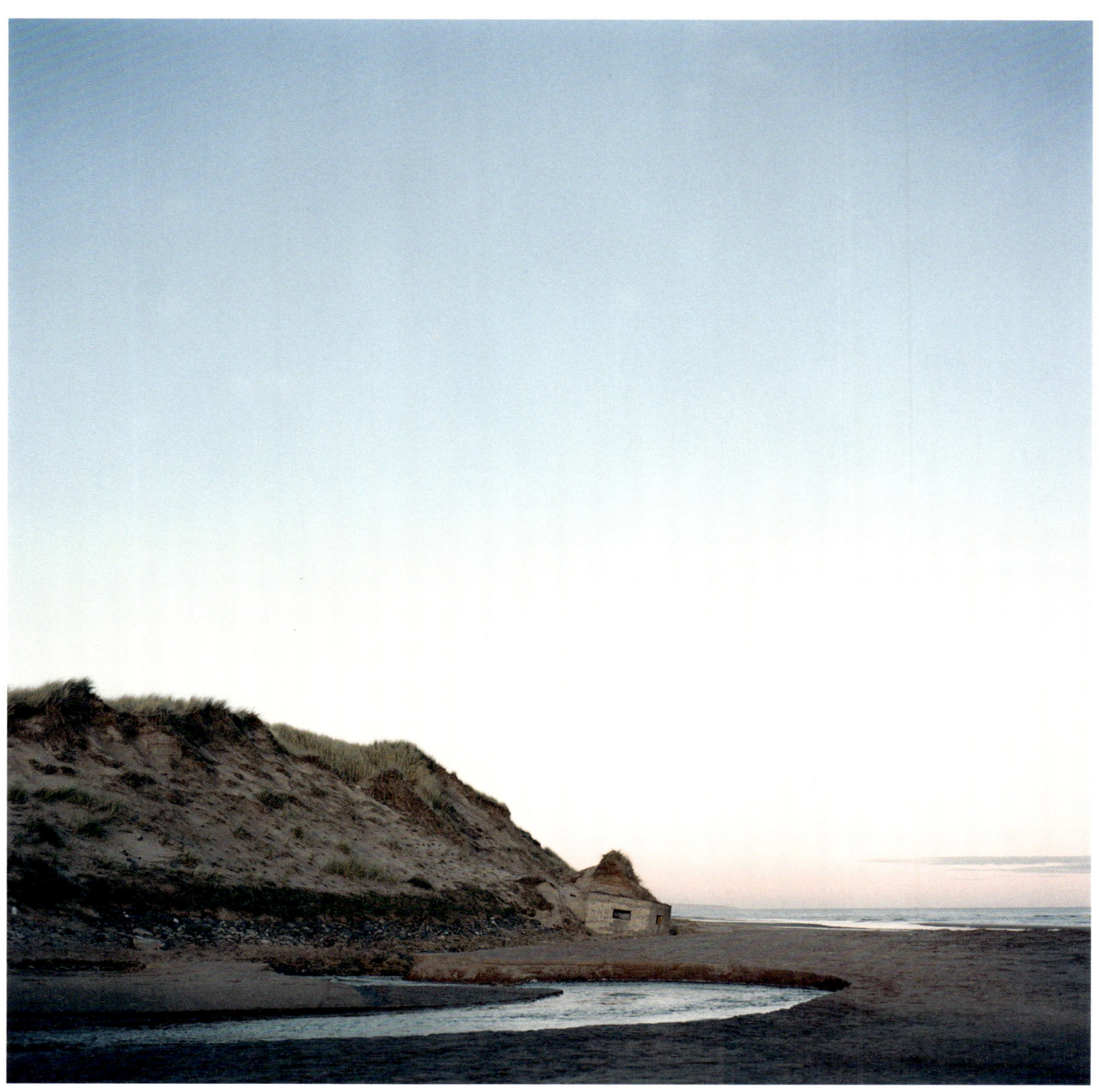

Blairton Burn, pre-2013.

I think the economic benefits of the golf course and the building and a hotel, if they go ahead, will be very substantial indeed. I'm disappointed that the plans haven't gone ahead as originally envisaged. I hope they will do.

—Alex Salmond, First Minister of Scotland, MSP for Menie, 2013

(Source: BBC Panorama's *The Trouble with Trump*)

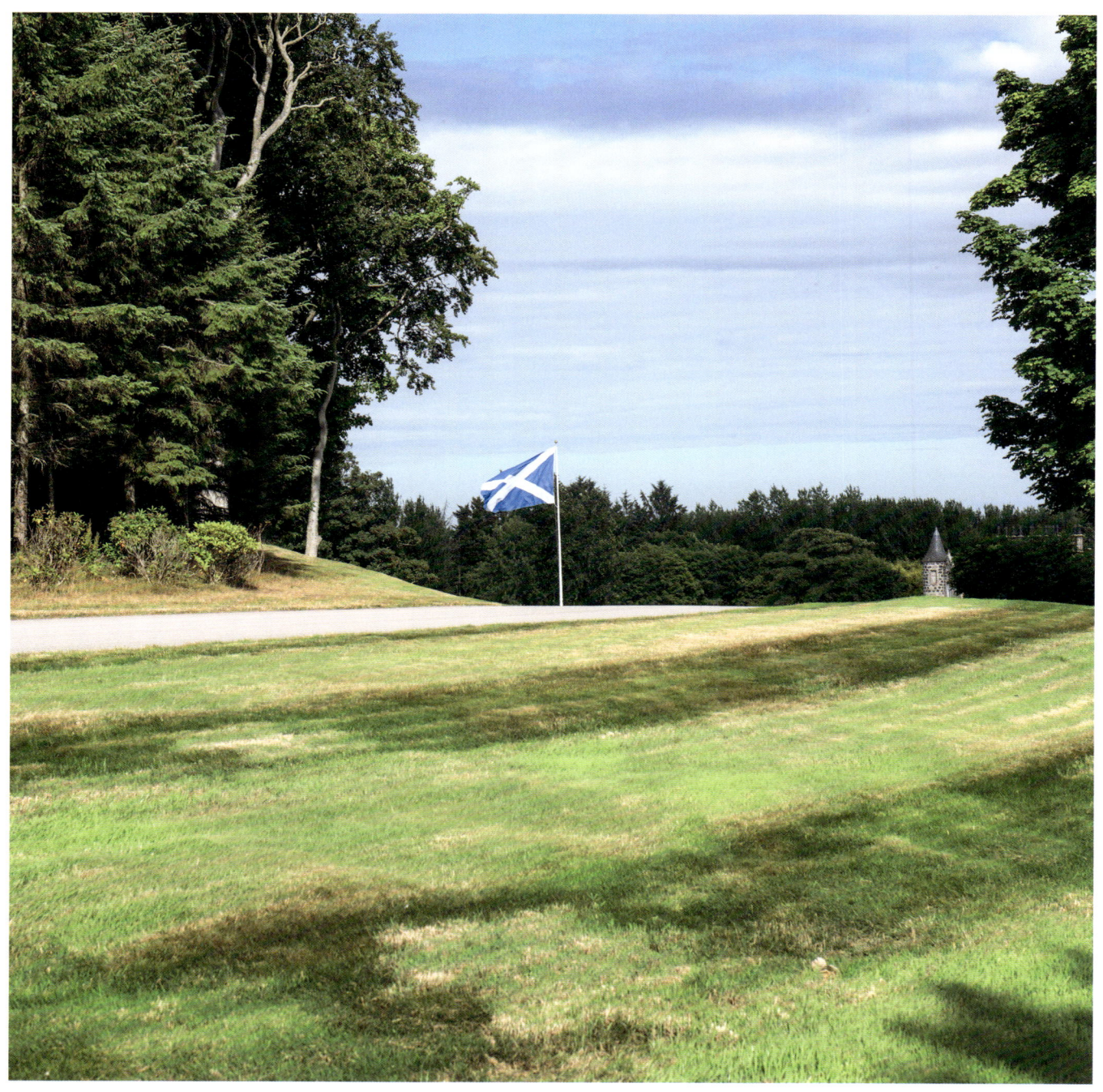

Arrival via Trump Boulevard to MacLeod House (previously Menie House), Donald Trump's Scottish residence as well as a rentable accommodation sleeping up to twenty guests, July 2022.

My family and I have lived in Leyton Cottage for nearly three decades. This is where we brought up our two boys, Murdo and Finlay. We've expanded our home over the years. When we moved in it was a but 'n' ben, but we saw the potential and, like everyone who visits Menie, we fell in love with the location.

There is now a large bank of sand and road in front of our home which obscures the view and stops us from seeing our neighbours, Mike, Sheila, and Molly.

I know Menie like the back of my hand: the wildflowers that grow, the way the dome moved, the beach; it's just absolutely gorgeous. You don't walk a dog every day for twenty-eight years without knowing every kink in the landscape.

Of course, now we can't get to the beach. Menie has become a building site. It breaks my heart. No one's going to have access to Menie; it's going to be a private development, and it doesn't seem to be about golf at all. It's about housing.

—Susan Munro, Menie resident, 2010

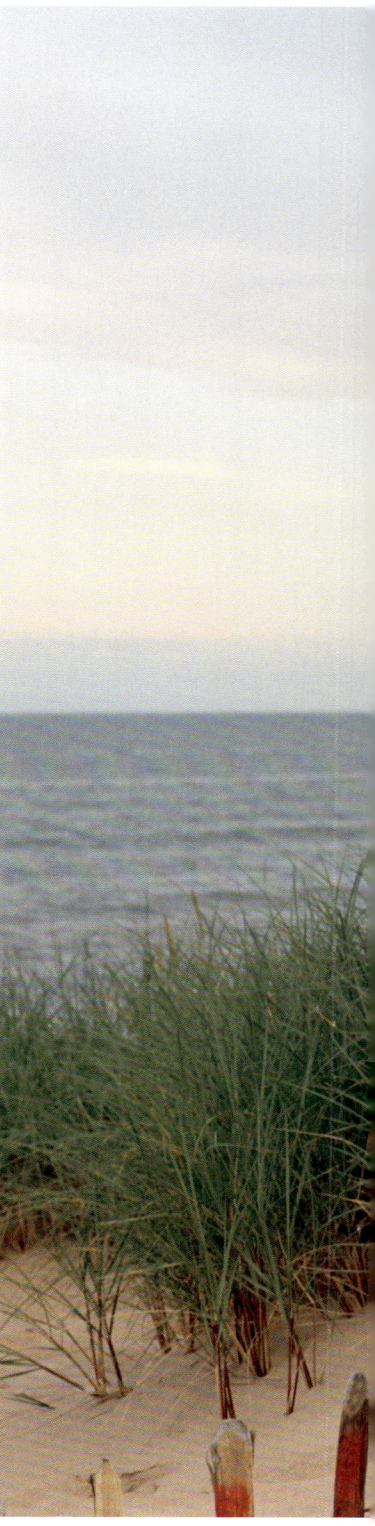

Susan Munro,
Leyton Cottage,
July 2010.

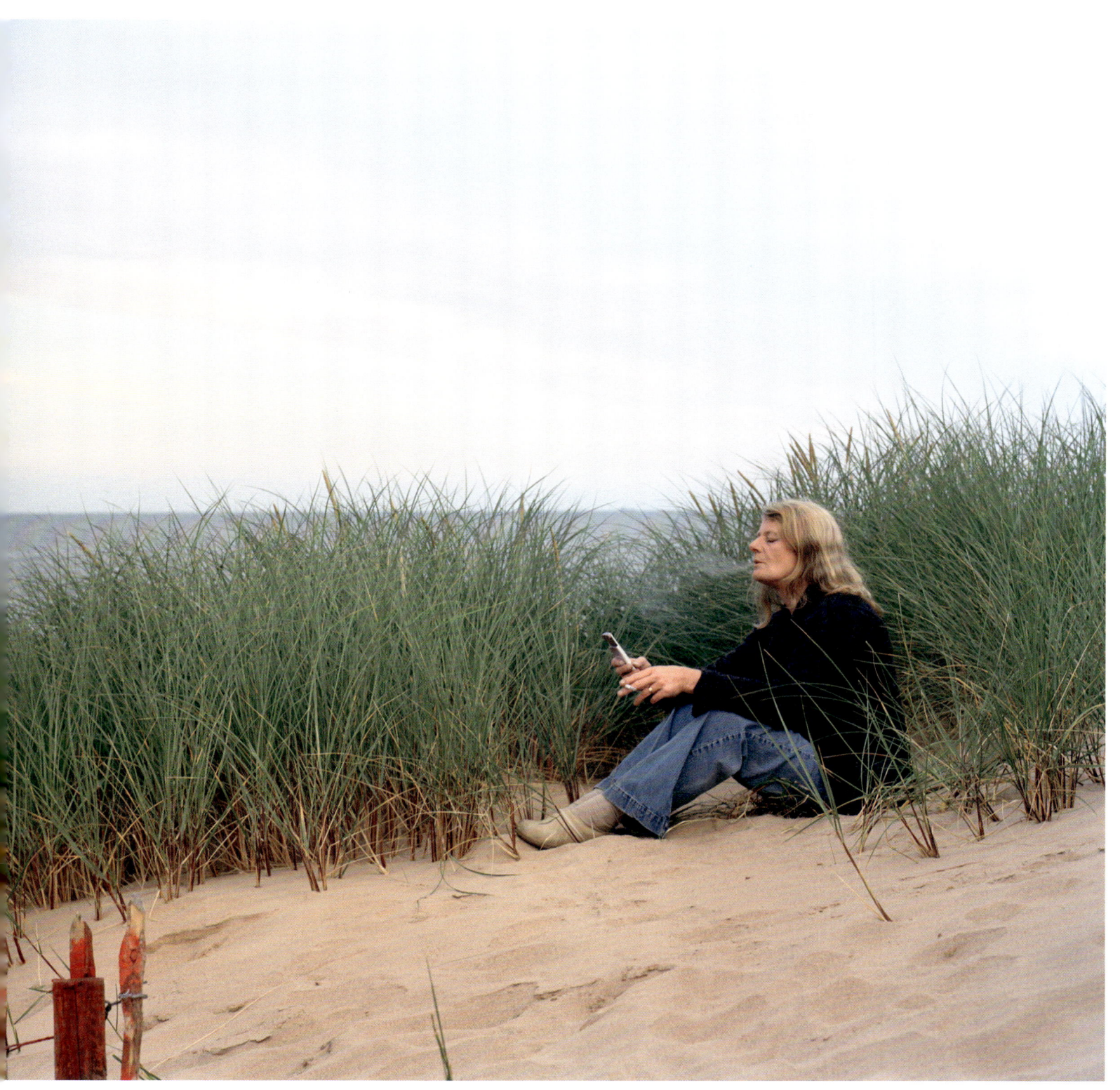

Molly Forbes is the biggest hero because she lived there for so long and Trump just wrote her off as an old woman. She was far more than that; she was everything that Trump wasn't. If you ever mentioned him, she would say, "That Trump, he's a horror." Her water was cut off. Seeing an elderly lady having to scoop water out of the burn with a bucket and wheel it round to her house in a wheelbarrow, that was ridiculous. She was houseproud, always dressed nicely, and looked after her chickens and her garden. For an elderly woman, she was amazing. She had absolutely no truck with Trump. She was hampered and fed up with people knocking at her door, and with Trump people trying to persuade her to sell up.

I'm sure, in Sheila [Forbes'] and Susan [Munro]'s case the aggravation, with Trump there all the time surrounding them, that it had something to do with their early deaths. There were high levels of stress.

I remember meeting Donald Trump outside the golf course when I'd been down to take the dogs on the beach; he was sitting there in a golf buggy with his entourage around him. I walked over to him and said, "Why do you have to try and ruin these people's lives?" I asked him if he would come to see what it was like behind the bunds at Susan's house. He said no.

The destruction of natural habitat really upset me. It should've been a haven for the wildlife. The wilderness now has this strip of green that's been carved out, with their pesticides and weedkillers and things. They must be fighting against nature all the time.

—Sue Edwards, Tripping Up Trump campaigner, 2023

Sue Edwards,
Tripping Up Trump campaigner,
Balmedie beach,
16 July 2022.

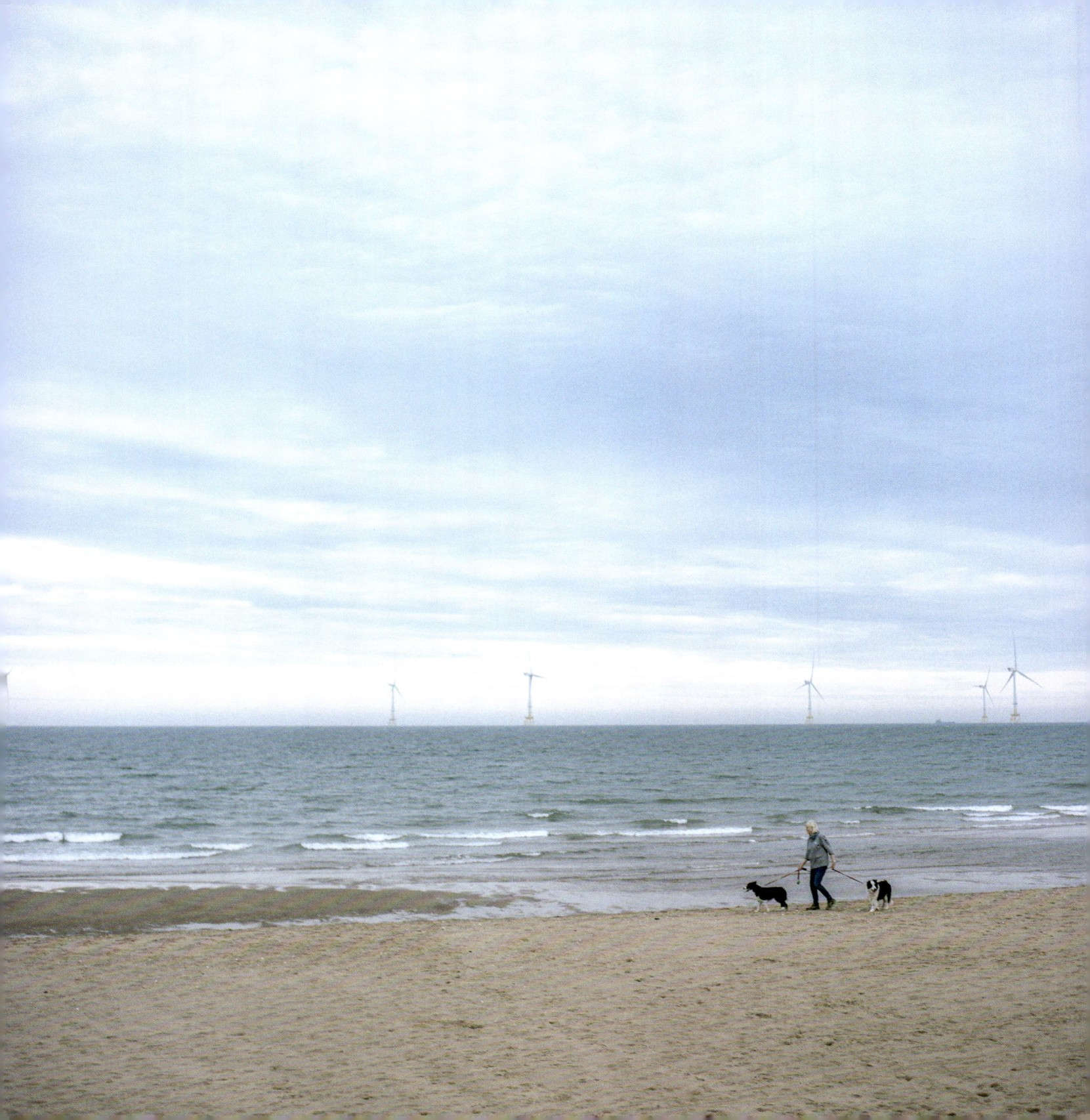

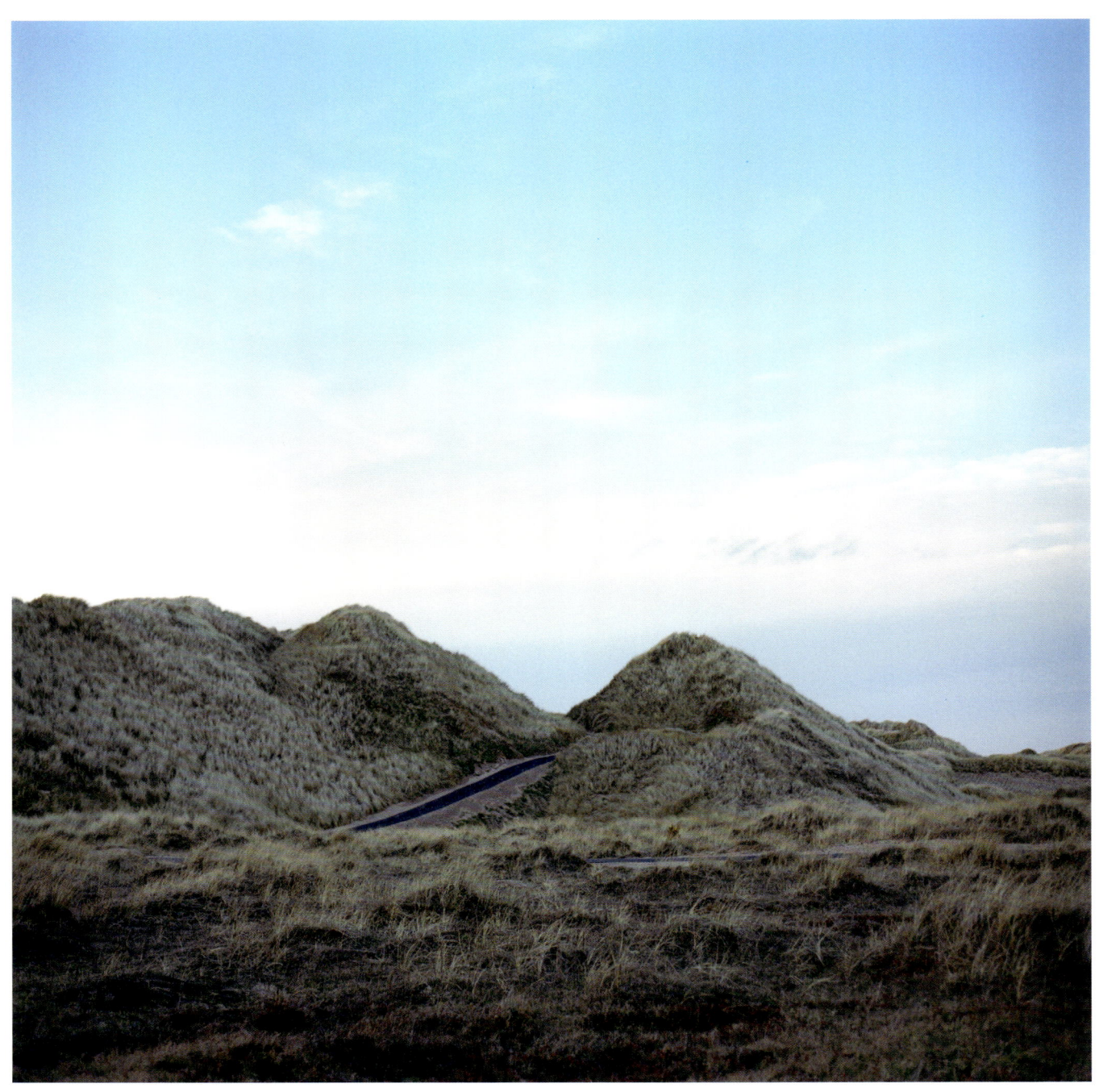

A black road resembling a scar on human flesh, laid during construction of Trump International Golf Links Scotland on the sand dunes at Menie, March–June 2011.

I've seen the northern lights from my doorstep. I've seen them every so often oot the back where we keep the hens, geese, 'n' horse. I stop for a while to look, then get back to whatever needs done. Where will we get another hame in a location like this?

Naewhere round here is as amazing.

I've stayed out the spotlight since this all kicked off. I just want to get on wi it wi nae hassle.

—Sheila Forbes, Menie resident, 2010

I've stayed here for 43 years; if I didn't like the place, I wouldn't have stayed so long. Ma history is doon here. All ma relations come fae roon aboot here and there's nothing mair magical than Menie. The wildlife is just ootside ma door, or was, till Trump came on the go. When the diggers are all working you dinna see the wildlife, but since the diggers are gone for Christmas holiday the wildlife is back.

The media's been camping on ma doorstep since 2006 but there's only certain media that prints the truth.

All I want is to be left in peace, the same as all the locals. Just leave me in peace. The only good thing this situation has ever done for Menie is brought all the locals together!

—Mike Forbes, Menie resident, 2010

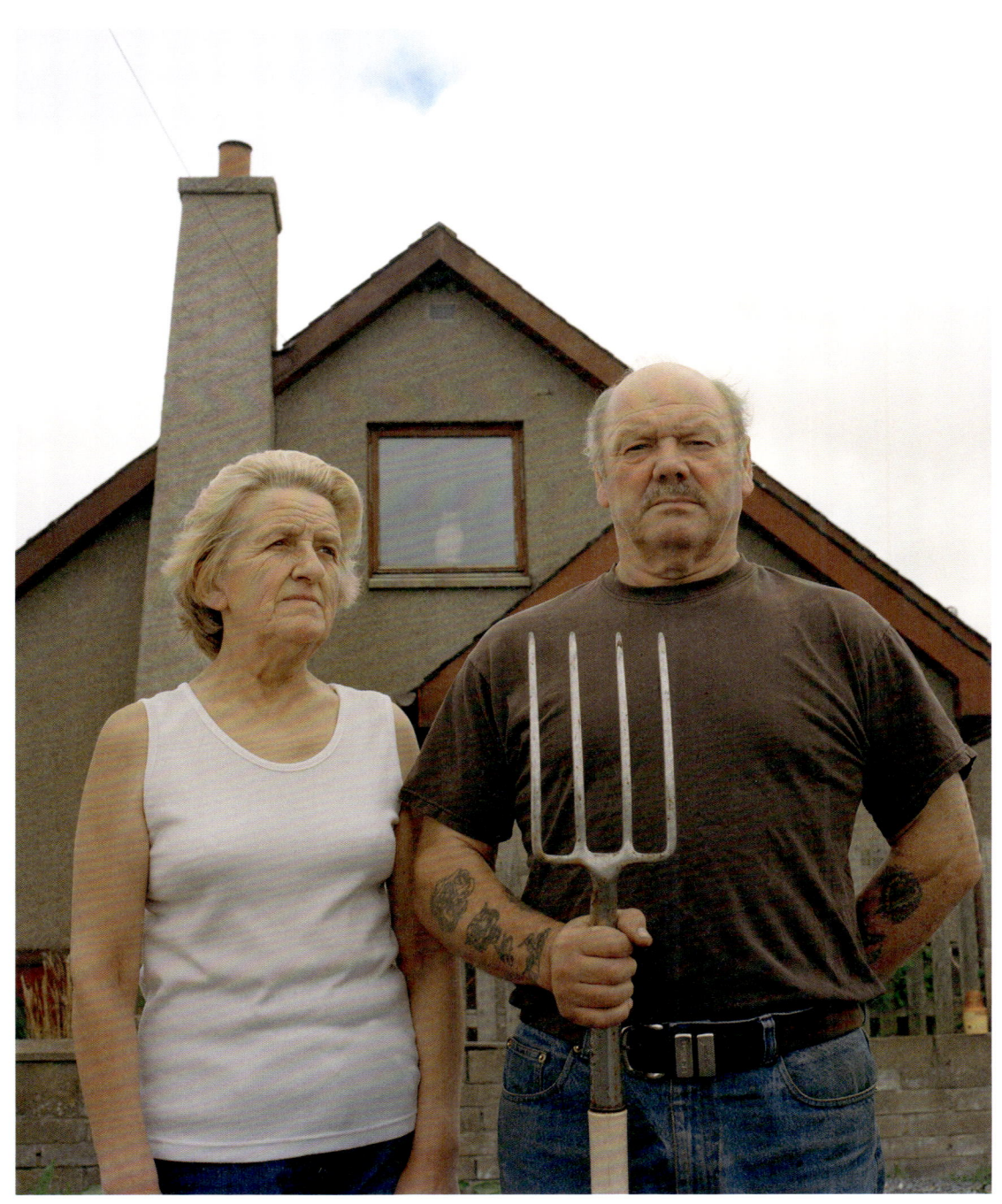

Mike and Sheila Forbes, Mill of Menie, 15 August 2010.

There are some houses quite far away from the course, but nevertheless, they are in view; but we are berming some of the areas so that you don't see the houses. I don't want to see the houses, and nobody has a problem with that. I guess maybe the people that live in the houses have.

—Donald Trump, October 2010

Leyton Cottage, the home of Susan and John Munro, surrounded by high mounds of earth and trees left by developers. The once-remote home previously enjoyed views out to sea and towards Aberdeen. This view from Hermit Point (David and Moira Milne's house) is no longer possible due to the number of trees that were planted in order to block the residents' view but also to hide the homes from the golfers' view; January 2013.

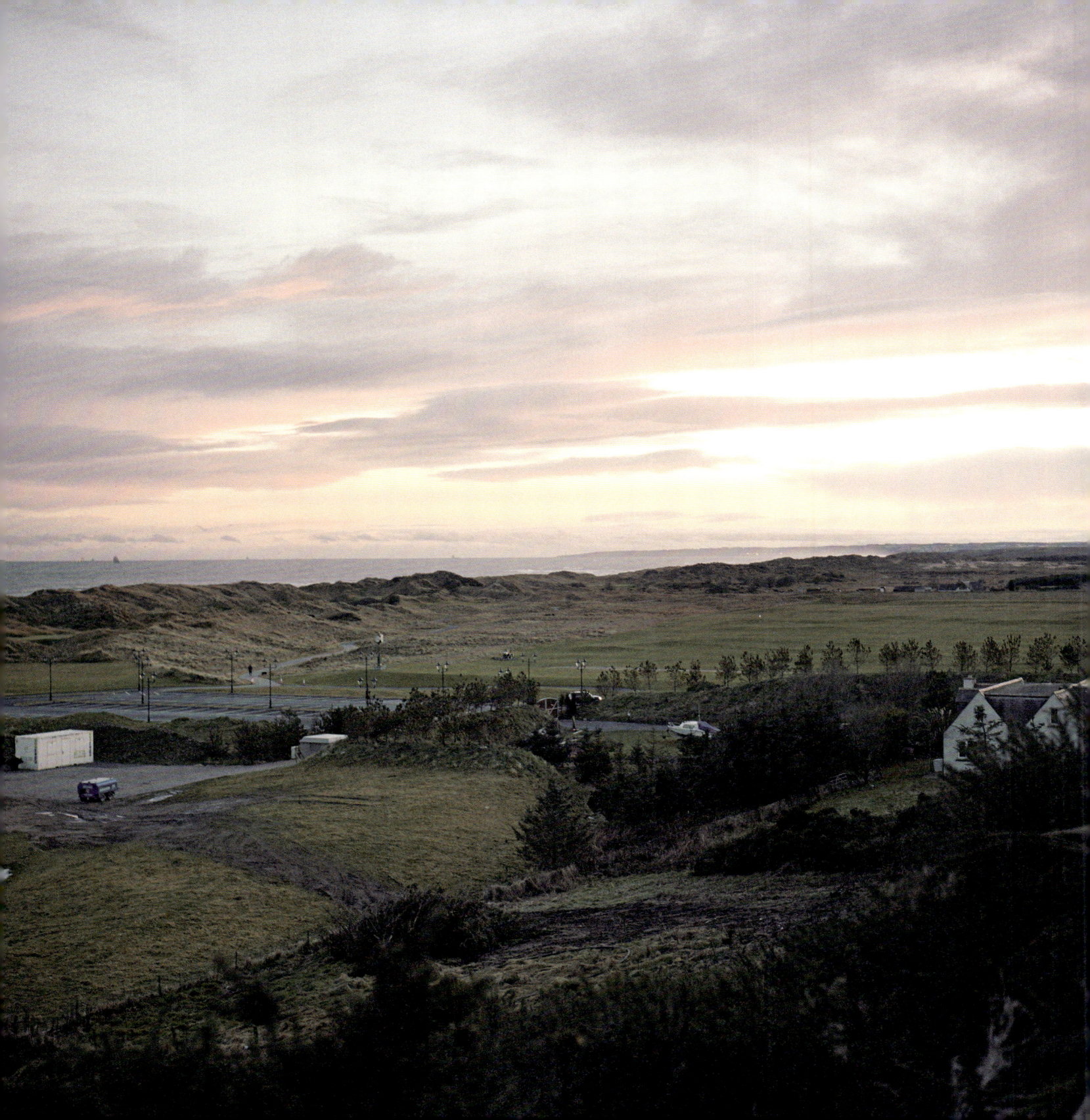

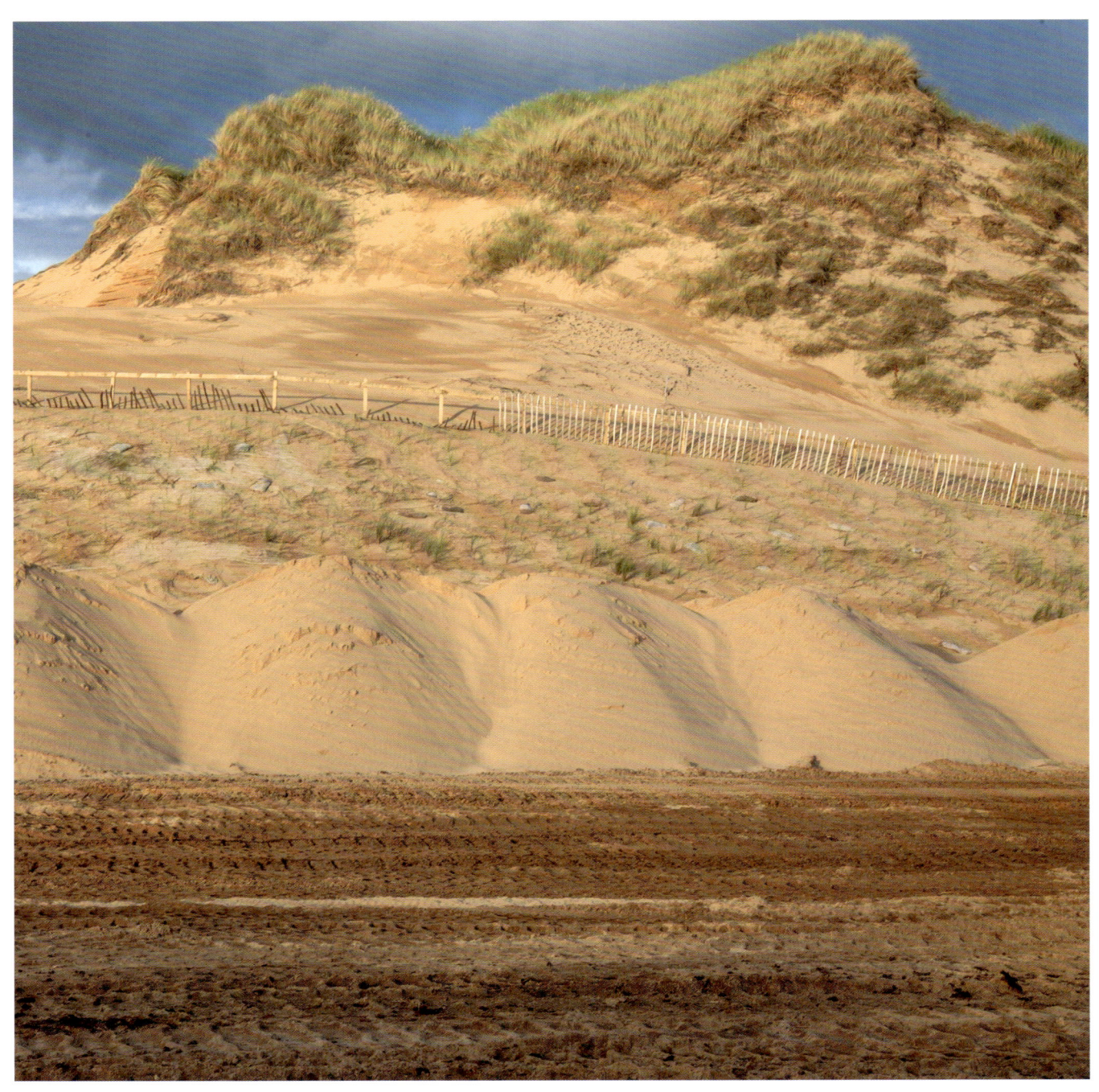

Construction underway at Trump International Golf Links Scotland, August 2010.

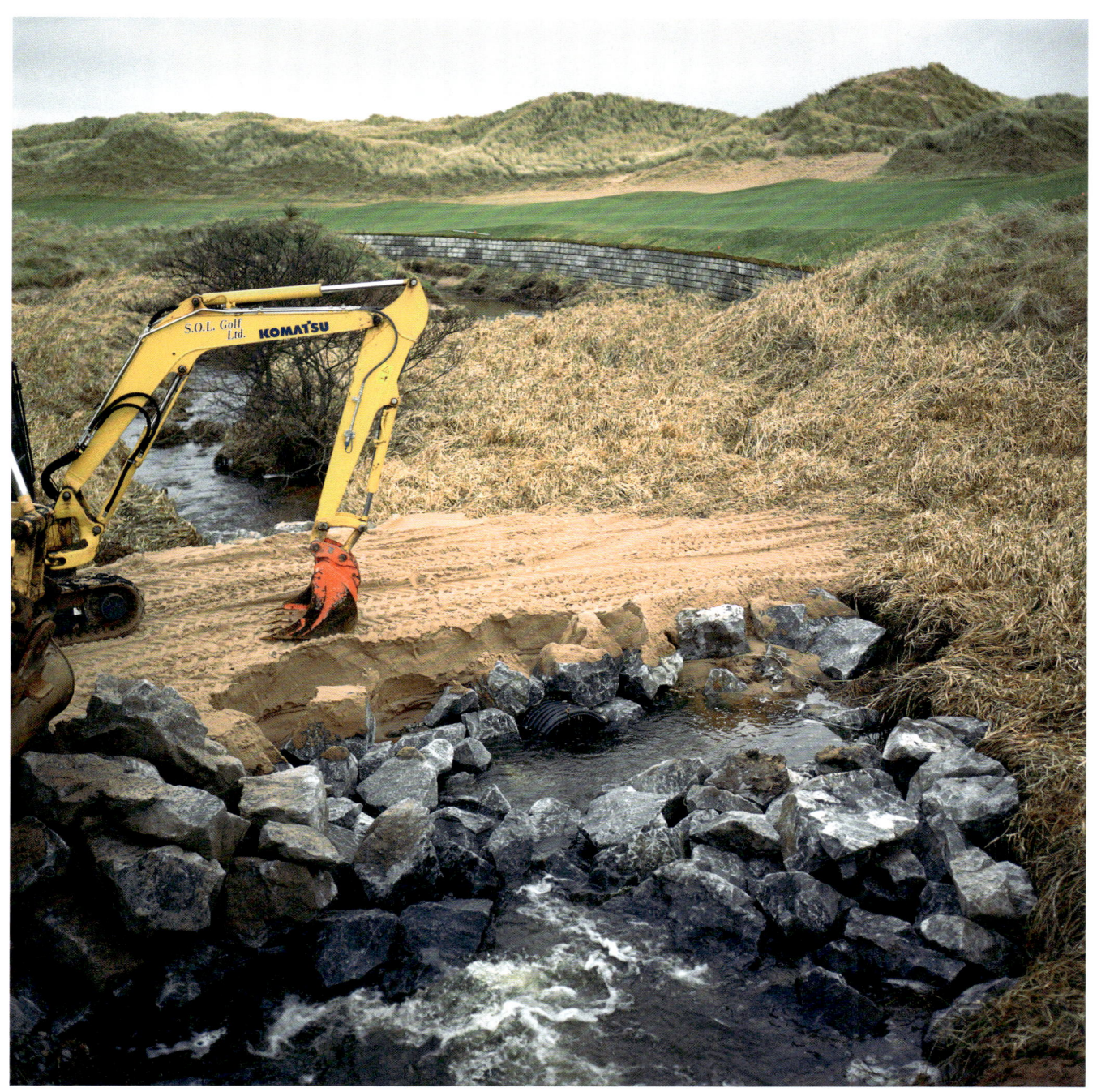

Construction and damming of Blairton Burn potentially causing course to collapse between third green and fourth tee, January 2013.

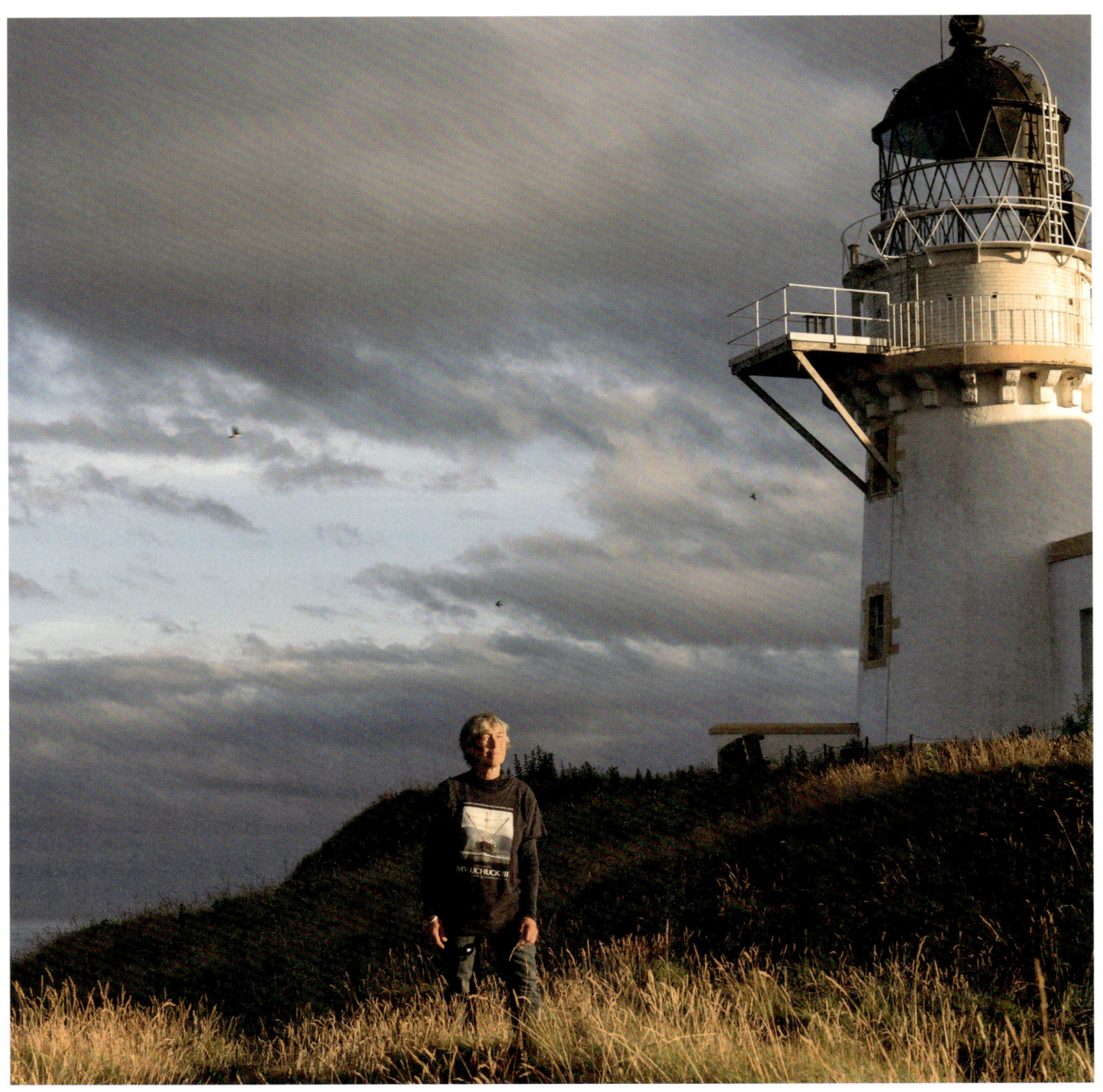

Rohan Beyts, Tripping Up Trump campaigner, Todhead Lighthouse, Catterline, 14 July 2022.

When I first heard that Trump was going to build a golf course on what was an SSSI, I thought it was an April Fools. My primary objection was to the destruction of the mobile dune system. I was walking in the dunes one day and needed the loo. I checked no one was in sight – I am very aware of the outdoor access code and made sure I followed the guidance on answering a call of nature outdoors. Three days later, just after 10 pm, the police came to my home and charged me under the Criminal Procedure (Scotland) Act. I was horrified, as I wasn't aware of anyone watching. I later found that I had been filmed not by CCTV, but by three men, two of whom were employees of Trump International Golf Links Scotland, one a newspaper photographer, and this added to my horror. I took a small claims action out against them but lost on a technicality. However, in his ruling the sheriff was highly critical of the actions of Trump Scotland, emphasising that any such action could be viewed as voyeurism. He also stated that he found me a credible witness who had acted entirely within my rights under access laws.

—Rohan Beyts, Tripping Up Trump campaigner, 2023

John Munro,
Leyton Cottage,
20 November 2010.

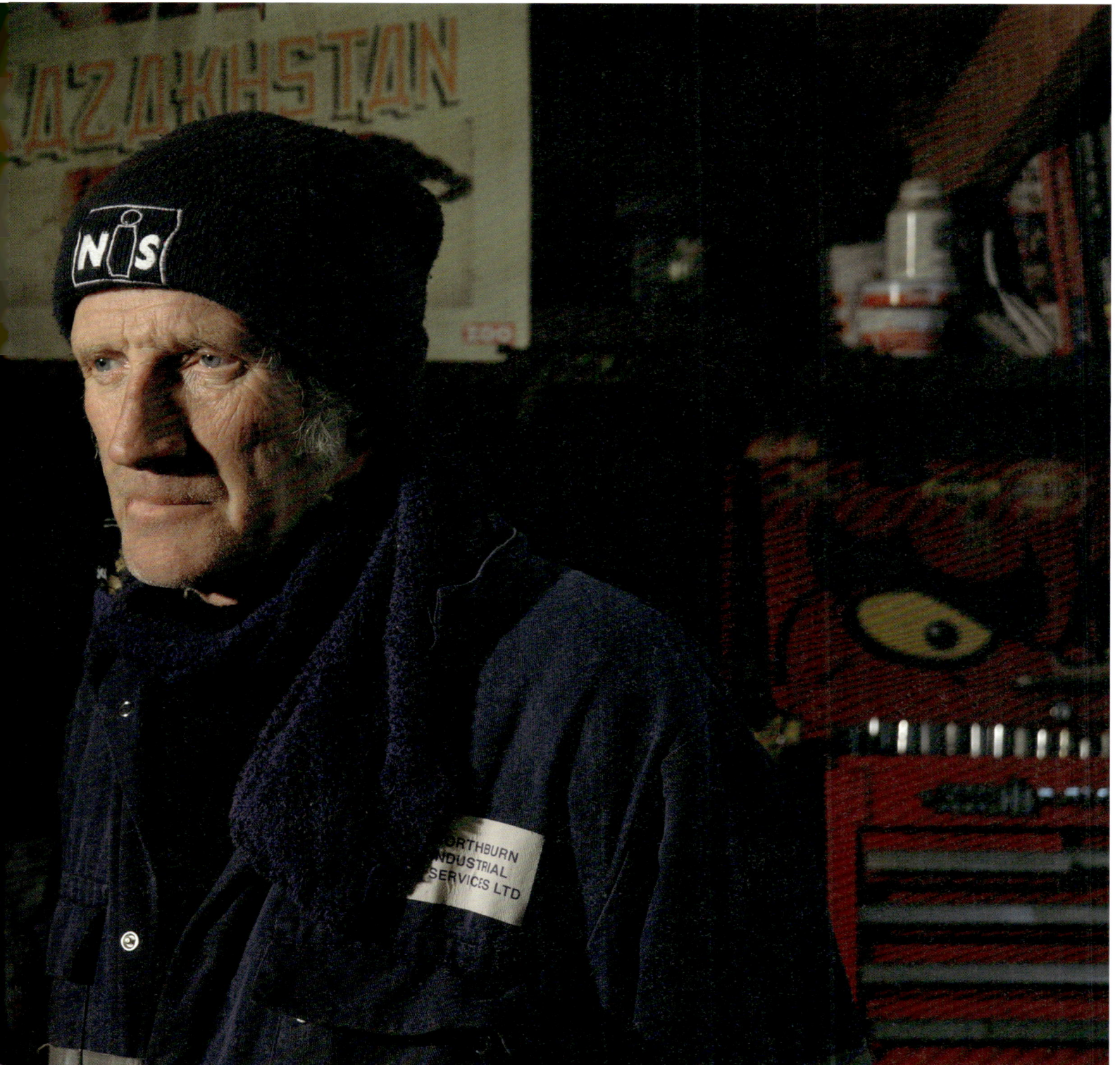

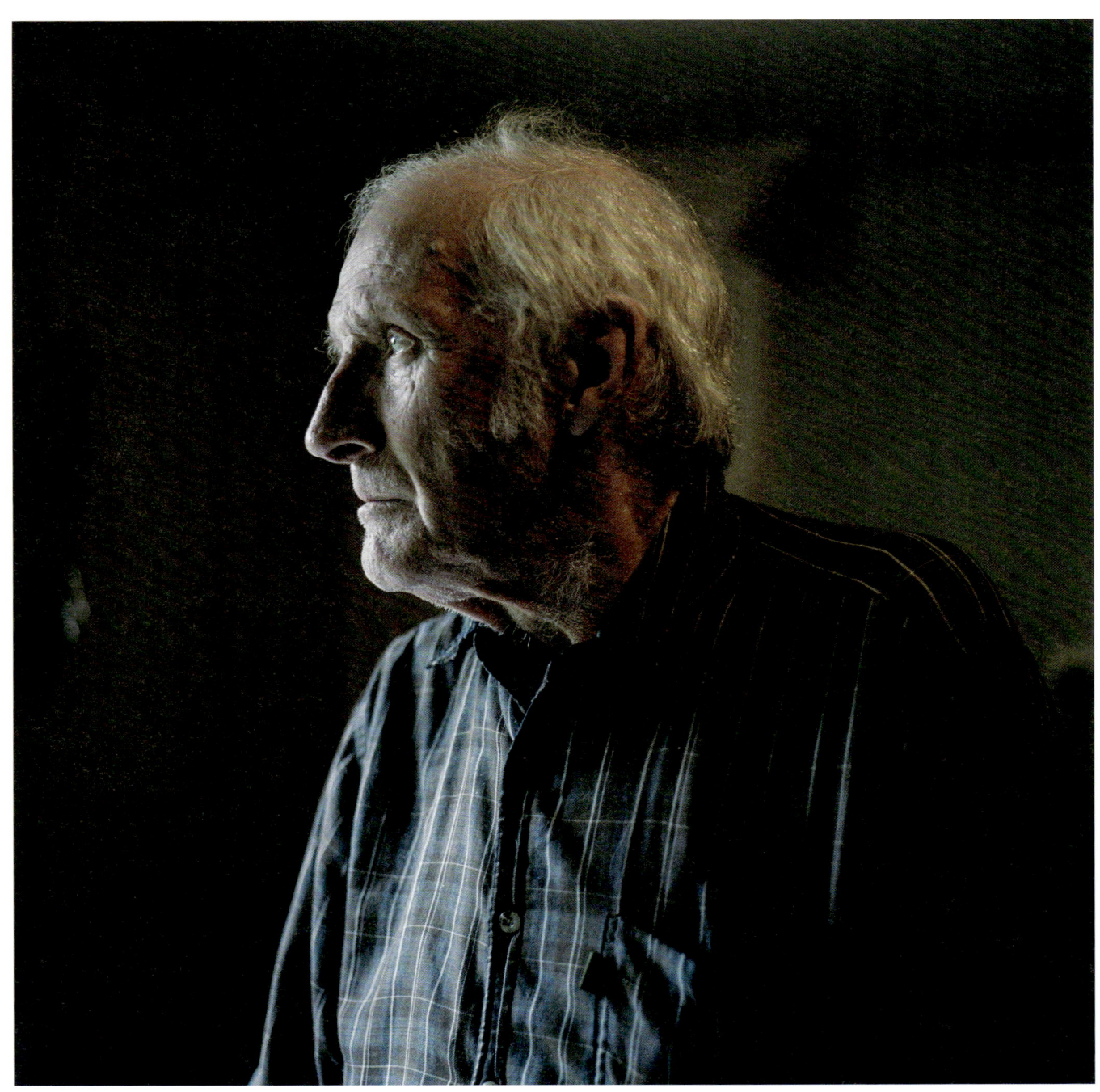

John Munro, Leyton Cottage, 23 July 2022.

I'm a man of few words. We aren't ragged-
trousered philanthropists here.

—John Munro, Menie resident, 2010

Land-use planning is about the appropriate use of land and buildings, and securing the orderly development of land in the public interest. The identity and motivation of an applicant for planning permission are generally not material considerations in deciding whether permission should be granted. What matters is what development is proposed. It is irrelevant if the applicant is Mother Theresa aiming to raise money to treat the sick, or some far from saintly person, or even Donald Trump.

—Martin Ford, local councillor

Trump Clubhouse car park,
Saturday, 23 July 2022.

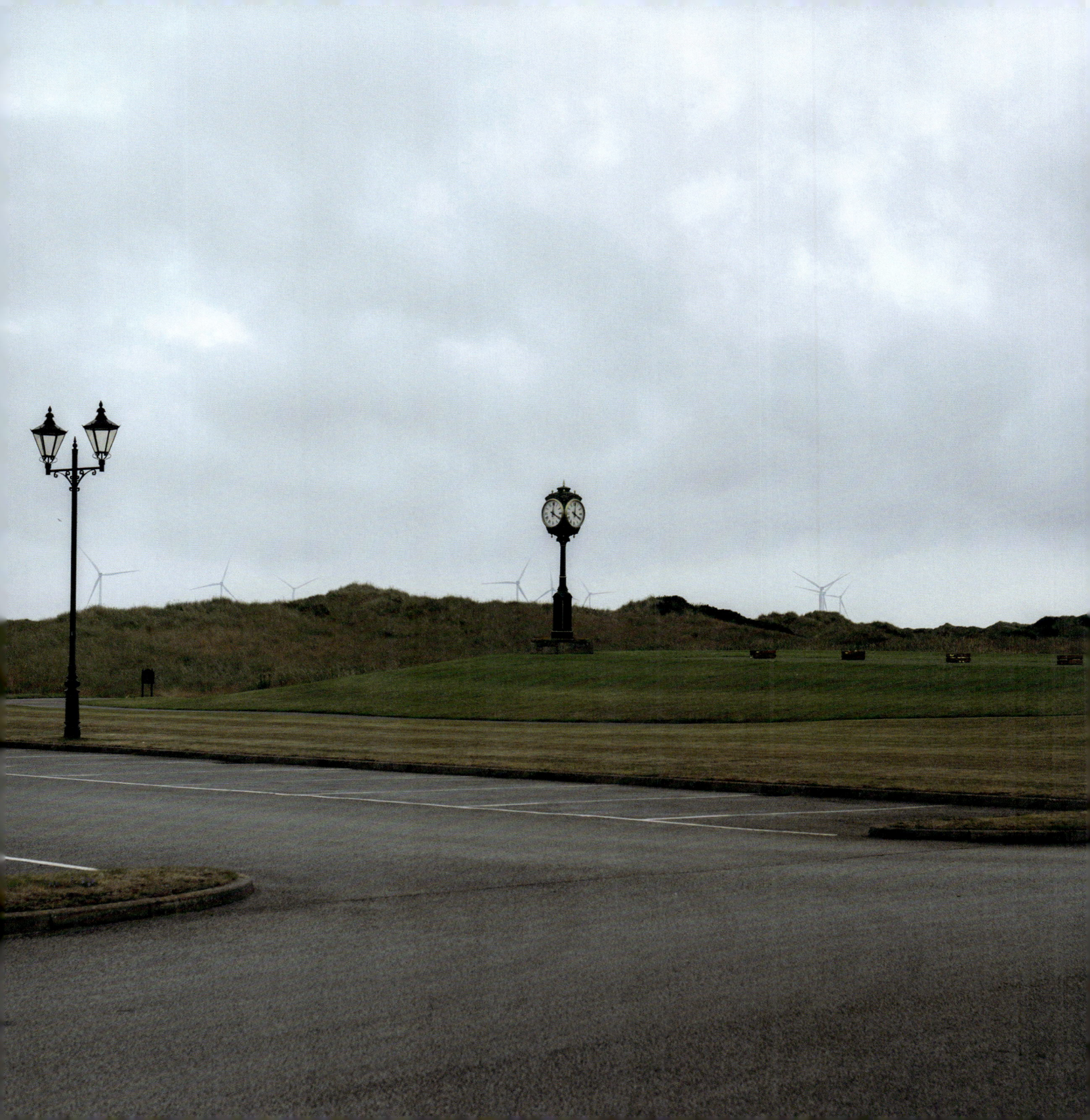

Haar (Scots for 'sea mist') on Balmedie beach near Blairton Burn and Trump's course, 2013.

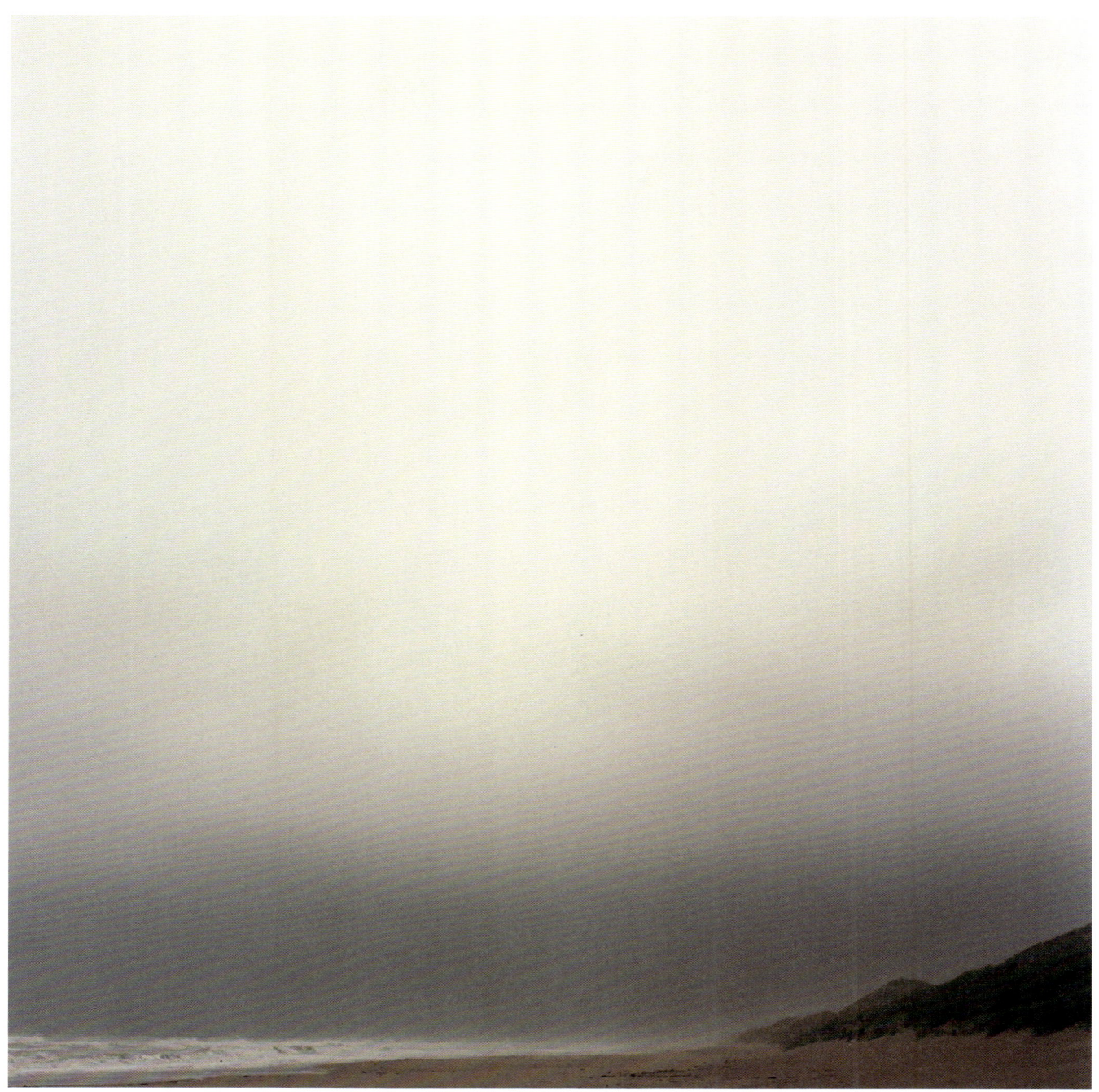

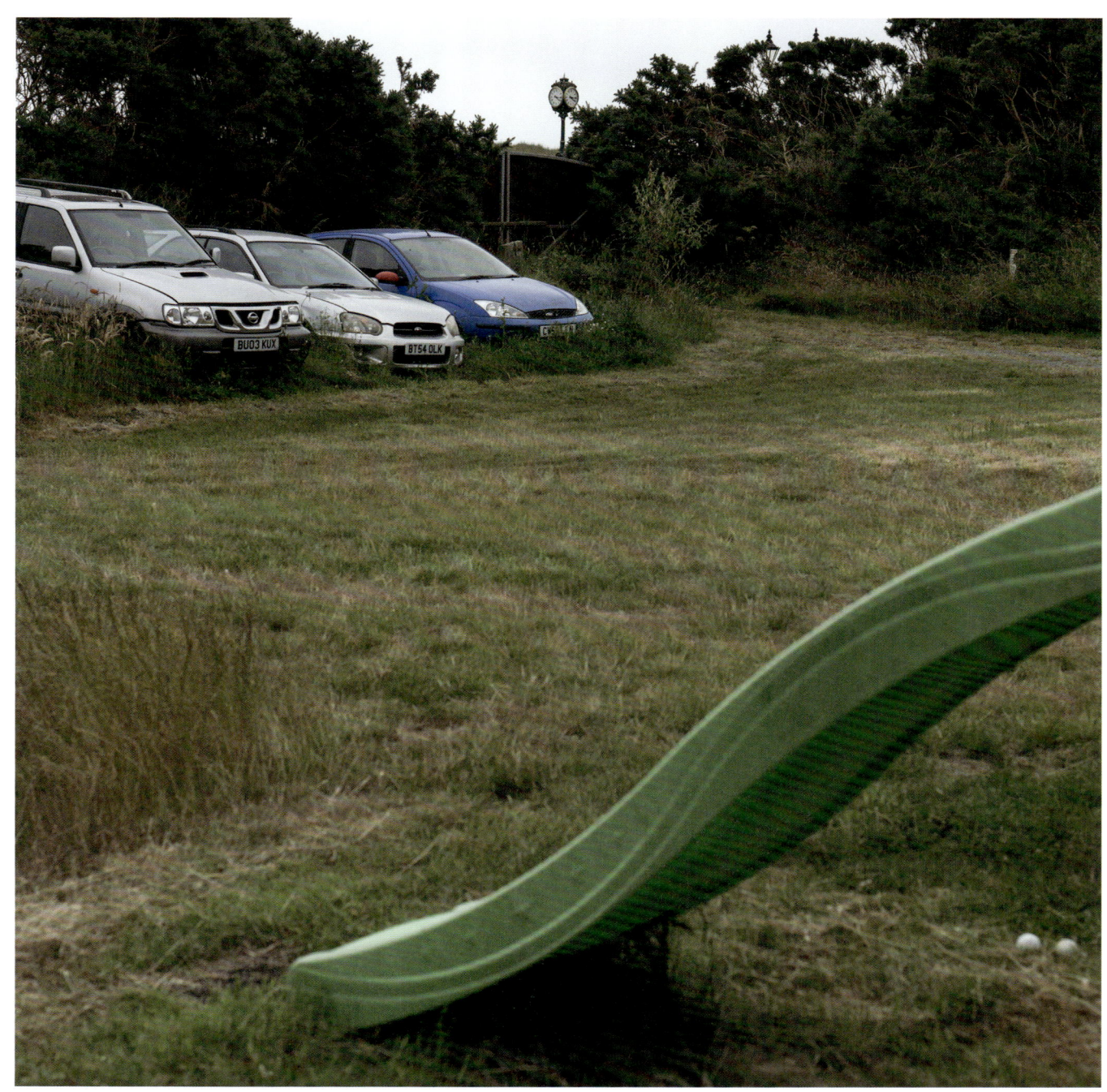

Golf balls landed on the grounds of Leyton Cottage, 23 July 2022.

John Munro,
Leyton Cottage,
23 July 2022.

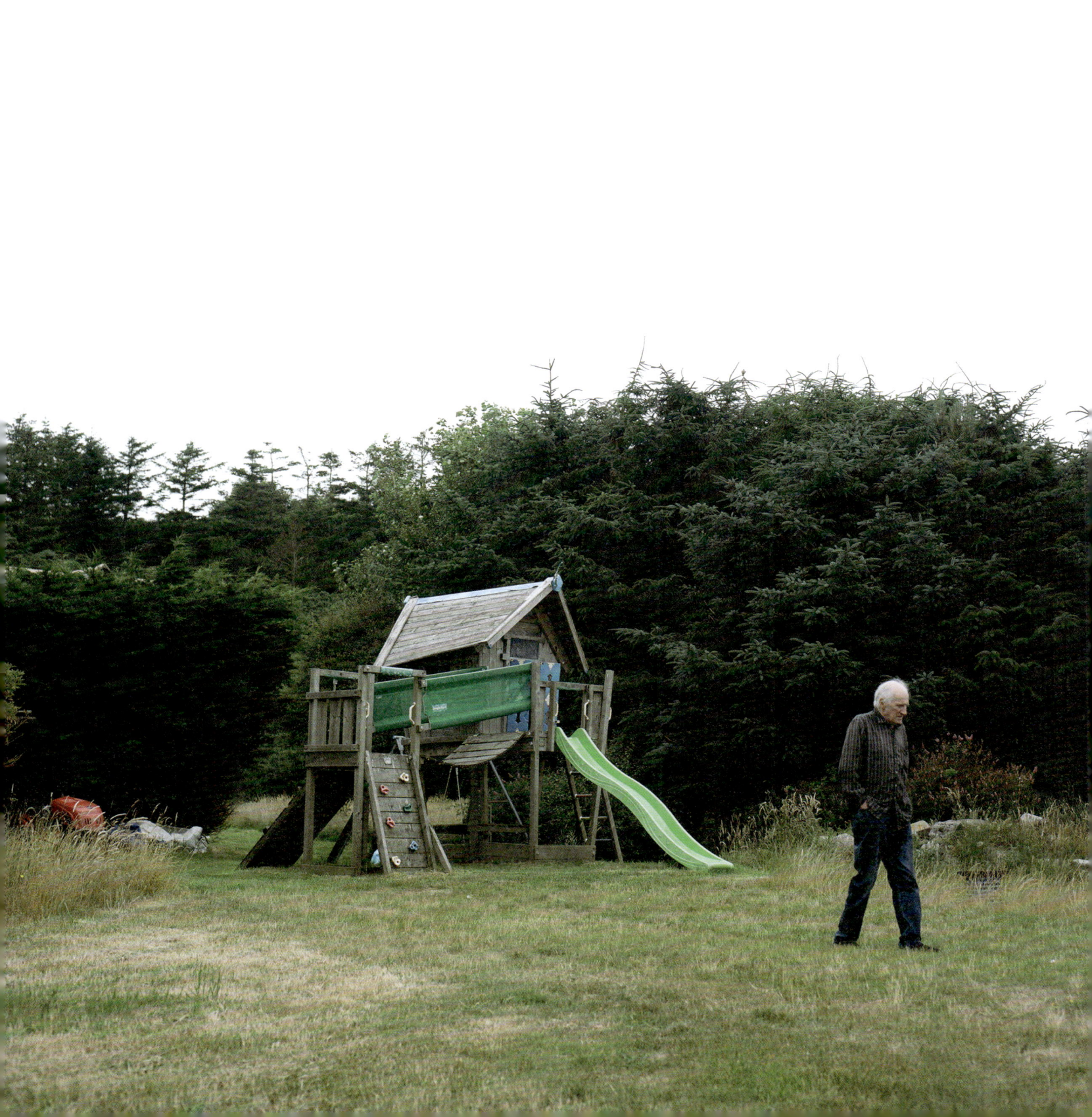

First and foremost, we're still here. We're not going anywhere, but we still keep an eye on the planning. In 1992, we bought this house as a coastguard station and converted it to a home. It was a phenomenal site, and we were led to believe that due to the Site of Special Scientific Interest (SSSI) [designation], no one would ever build on it.

Trump's presidency made America a laughing stock. He promises you the earth, and then gives you a handful of mud and tells you that's what he promised you. He is willing to lie, even on camera, even about his huge discrepancy of wealth. The press has almost been a malevolent presence, especially the local media, *Aberdeen Journals*, because they had shown that they were biased.

My first encounter with the Trump representatives was a phone call from Peter Boyd. He stated that he had been shooting on the Menie Estate and had fallen in love with the place. He wanted to buy a holiday home. Were we interested in selling? We were offered £100,000 for our property. He had the door shut in his face. Peter Boyd turned out to be Neil Hobday working for Trump, and he asked the same question of everyone in the area. The level of trust in the organization had already gone.

I raised a Mexican flag on my land in response to Trump talking about building a wall on the Mexico and US border; he was going to make Mexicans pay for it. That sounded familiar because he set a boundary, stuck up a cheap fence round us, and tried to bill us for it. We've also had trees planted around us to block our views, and our water cut off. You could see our flagpole from the golf course. We got messages from Mexico, including offers of replacement flags when required.

—David Milne, Menie resident, 2023

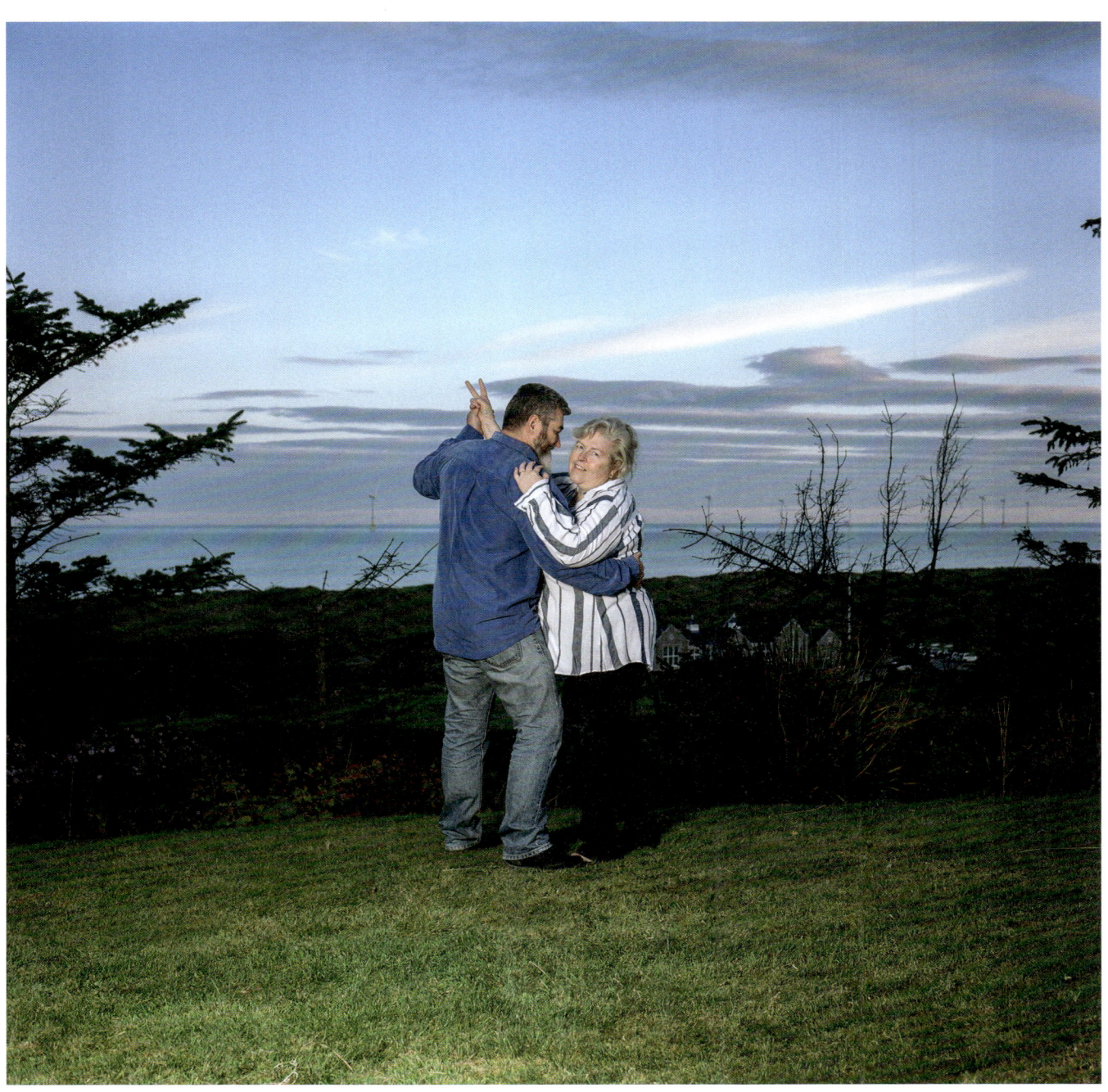

David and Moira Milne, Hermit Point, 2022.

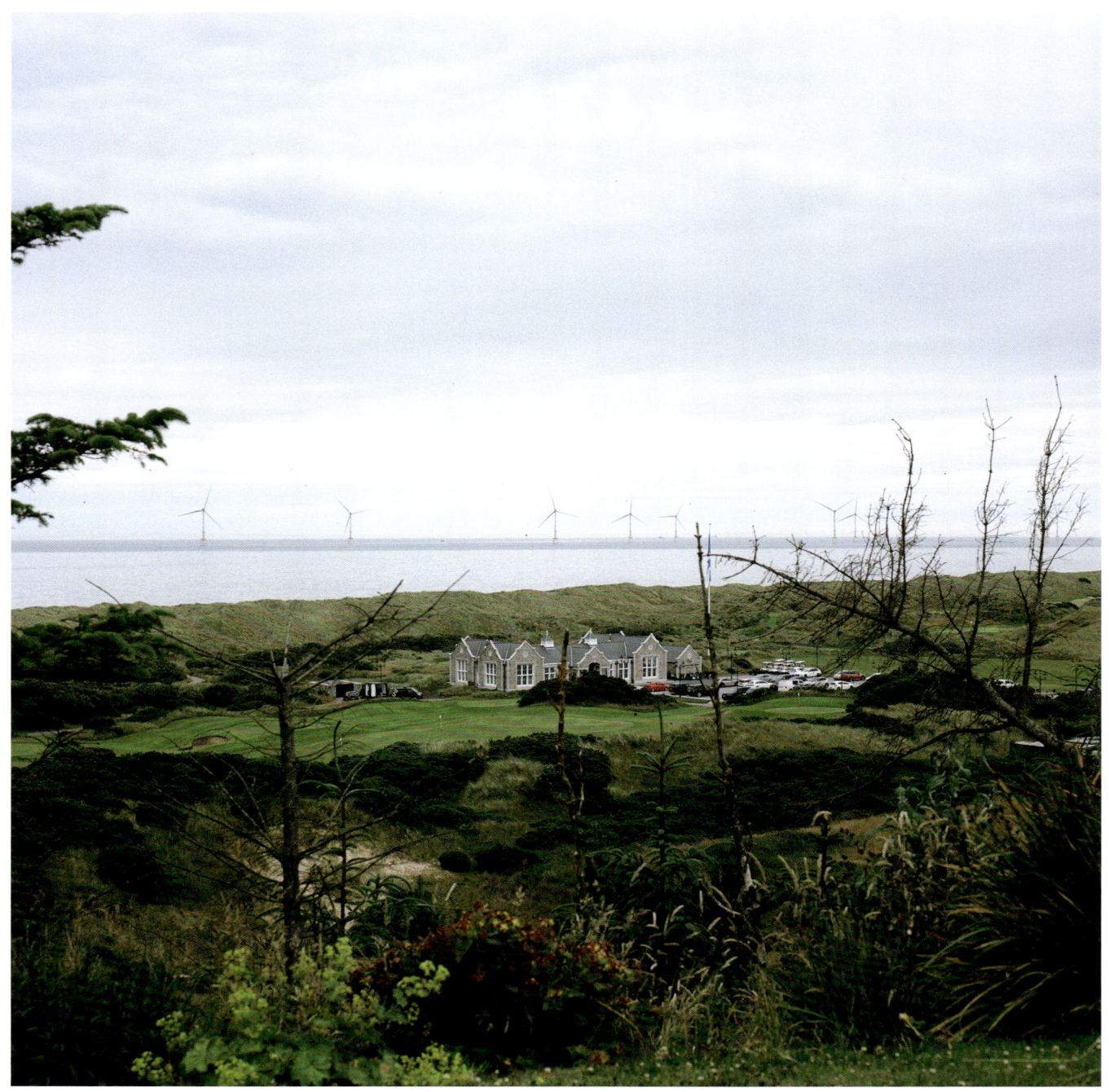

Trump Clubhouse and Aberdeen Bay wind turbines in the North Sea with salt- and storm-damaged trees surrounding the boundary of Hermit Point, the home of David and Moira Milne, 12 September 2021.

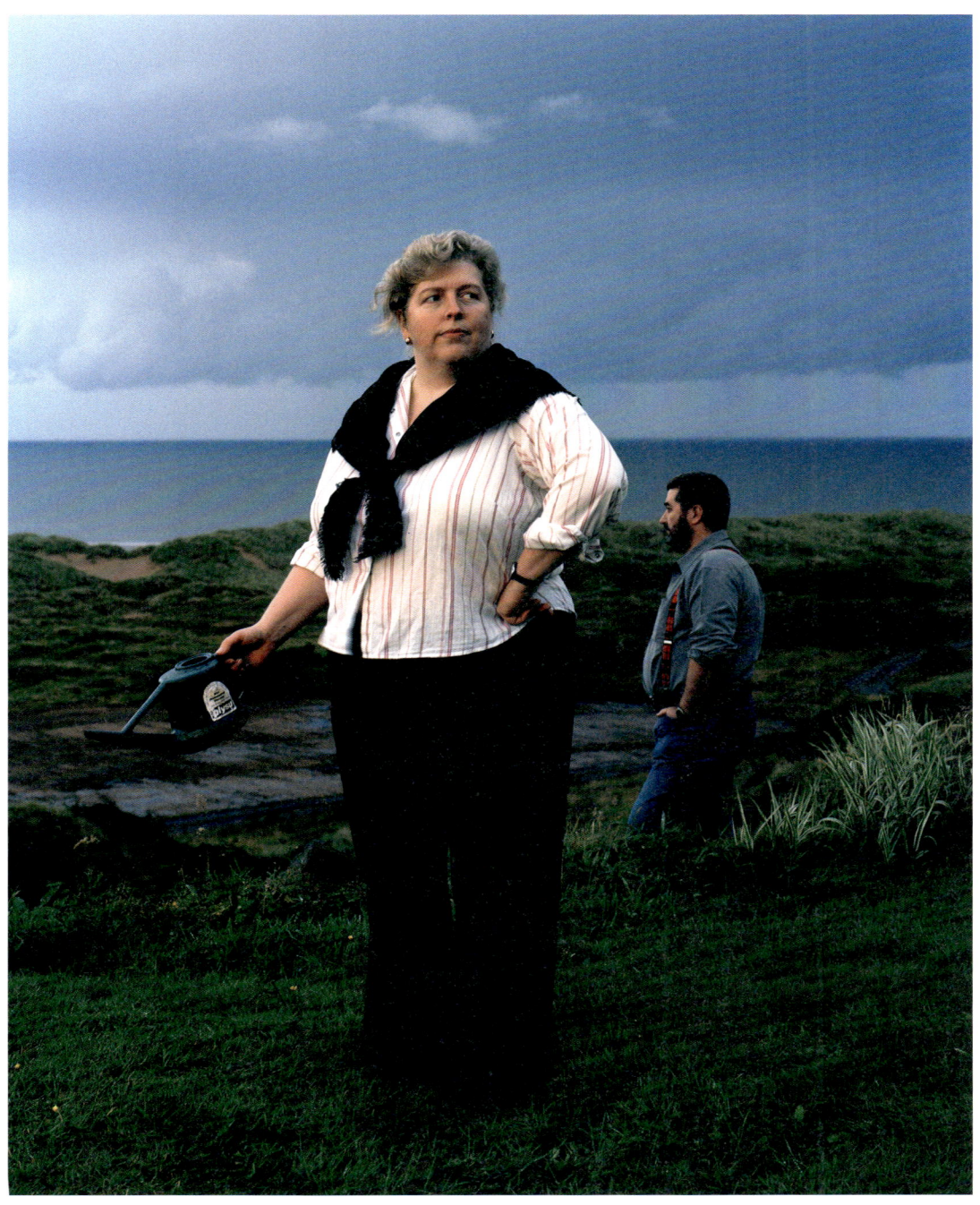

Moira Milne, Hermit Point, 19 August 2010.

The actual destruction of this area was brought home to me one day when bulldozers arrived and ripped out the young wood directly in front of my home. The waste of it all was that they were taken away on trucks to further south on the estate and just buried in a hole that they [the developers] had dug the previous day.

They now have problems with water lying there and they wonder why; trees drink lots of water.

This is just one example of the destruction. They also wish to destroy my home, which my husband and myself have spent years extending through our married life and has become part of us; it's like our baby. We have built it with our own hands; it has our blood, sweat, and tears in the walls. It's part of us and cannot be replaced, as it is a one-off, like each and every person is.

—Moira Milne, Menie resident, 2010

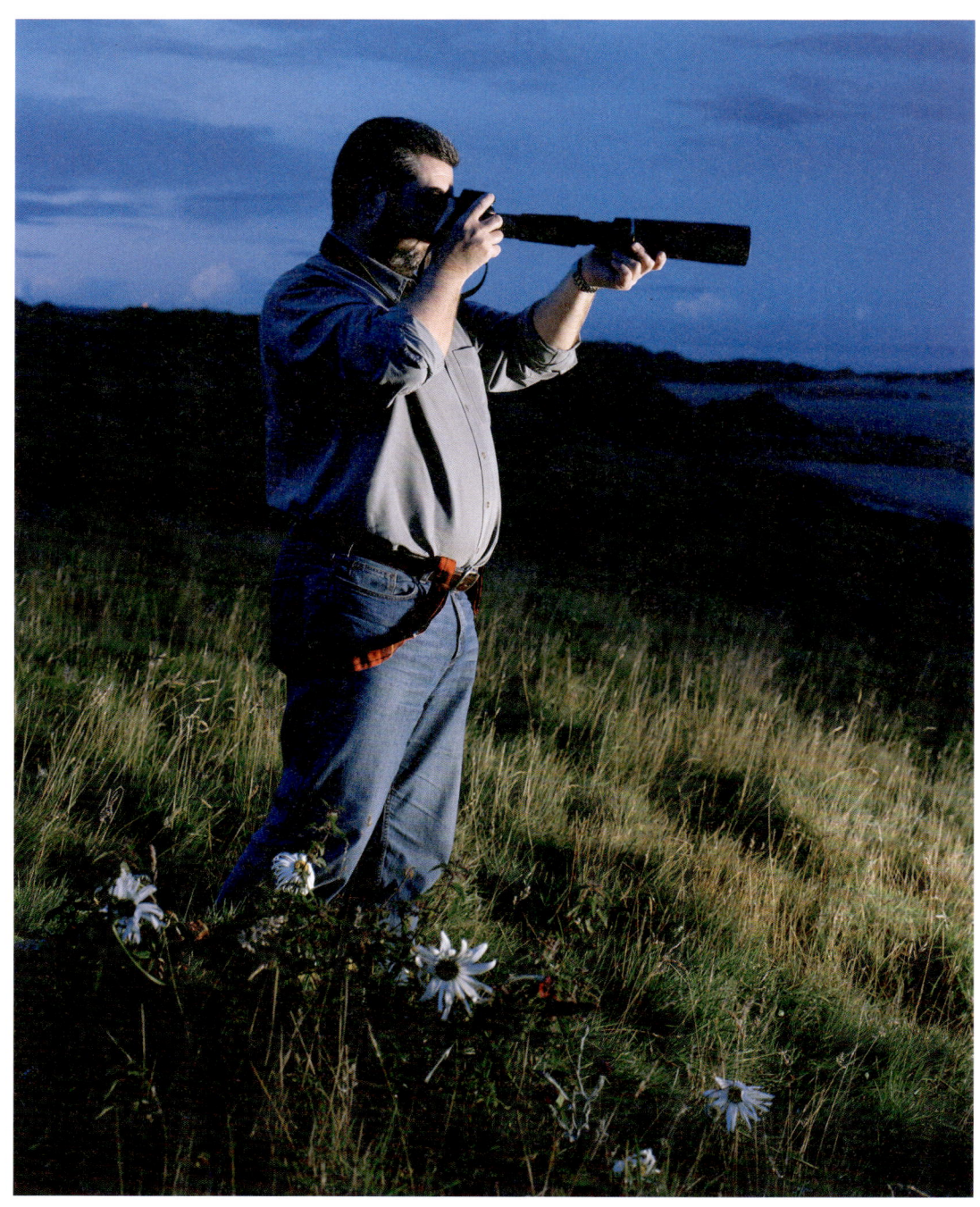

David Milne, Hermit Point, 22 August 2010.

End of the tarmac road,
March–June 2011.

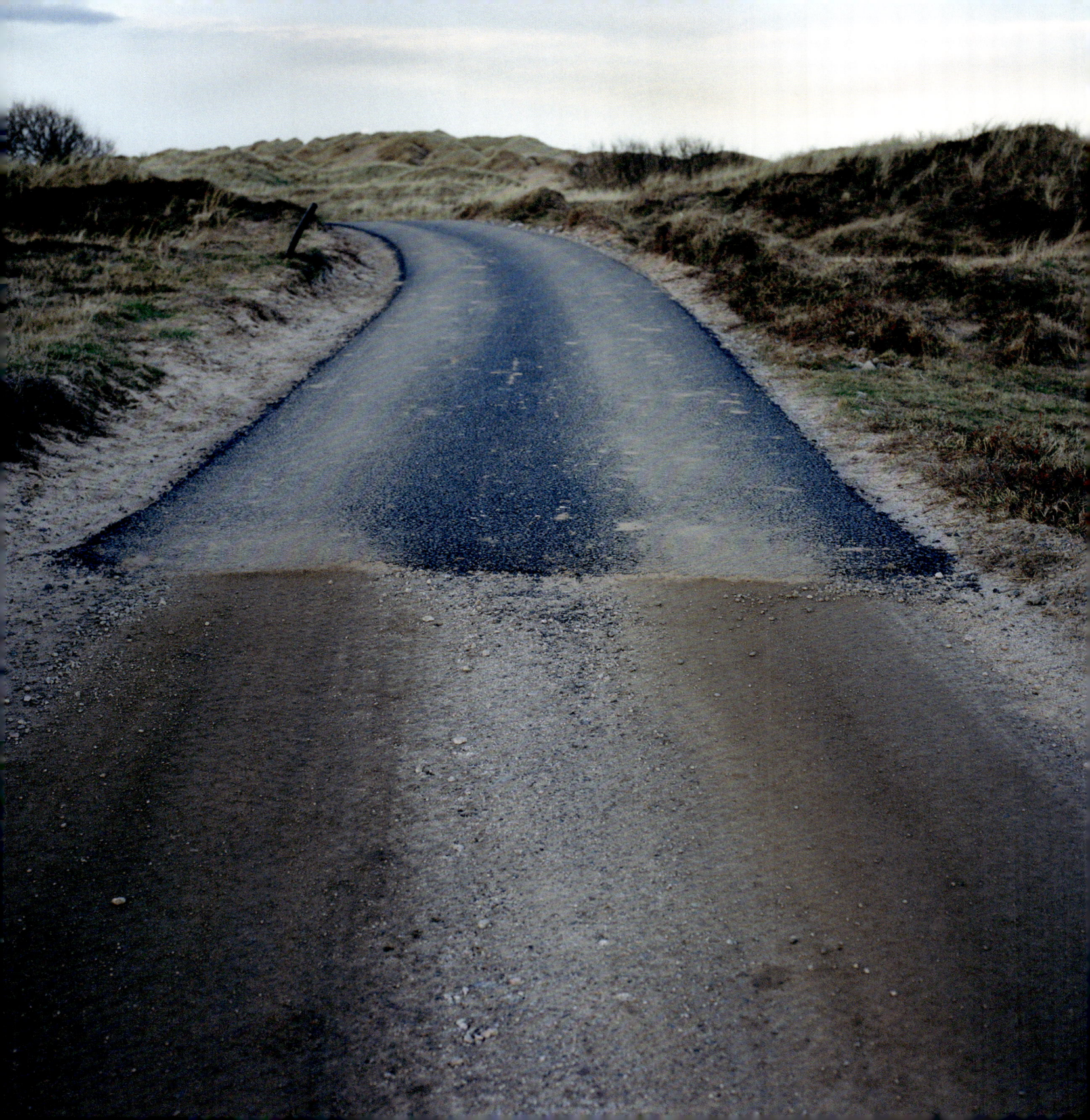

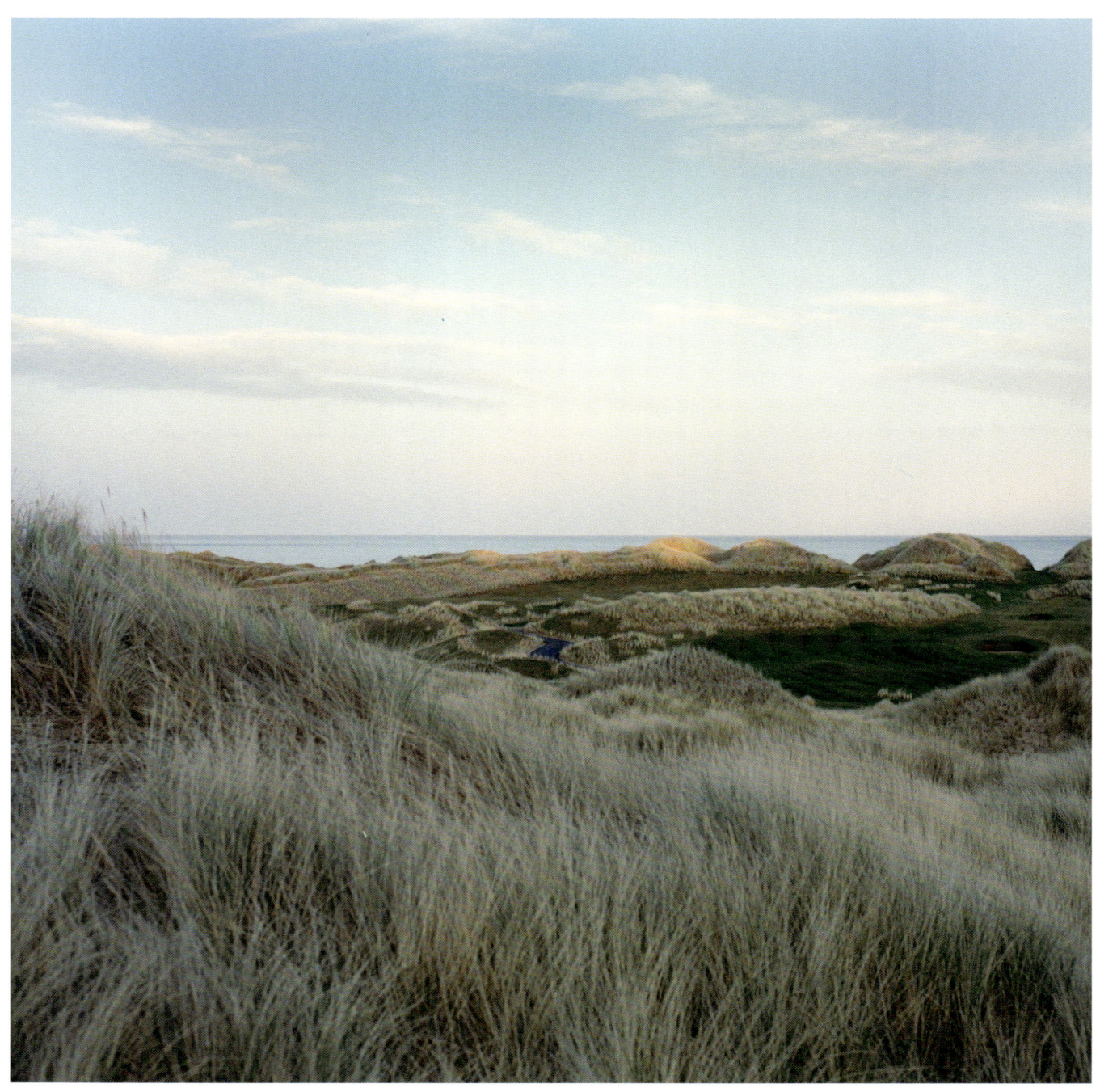

View over Trump International Golf Links Scotland, late spring 2012.

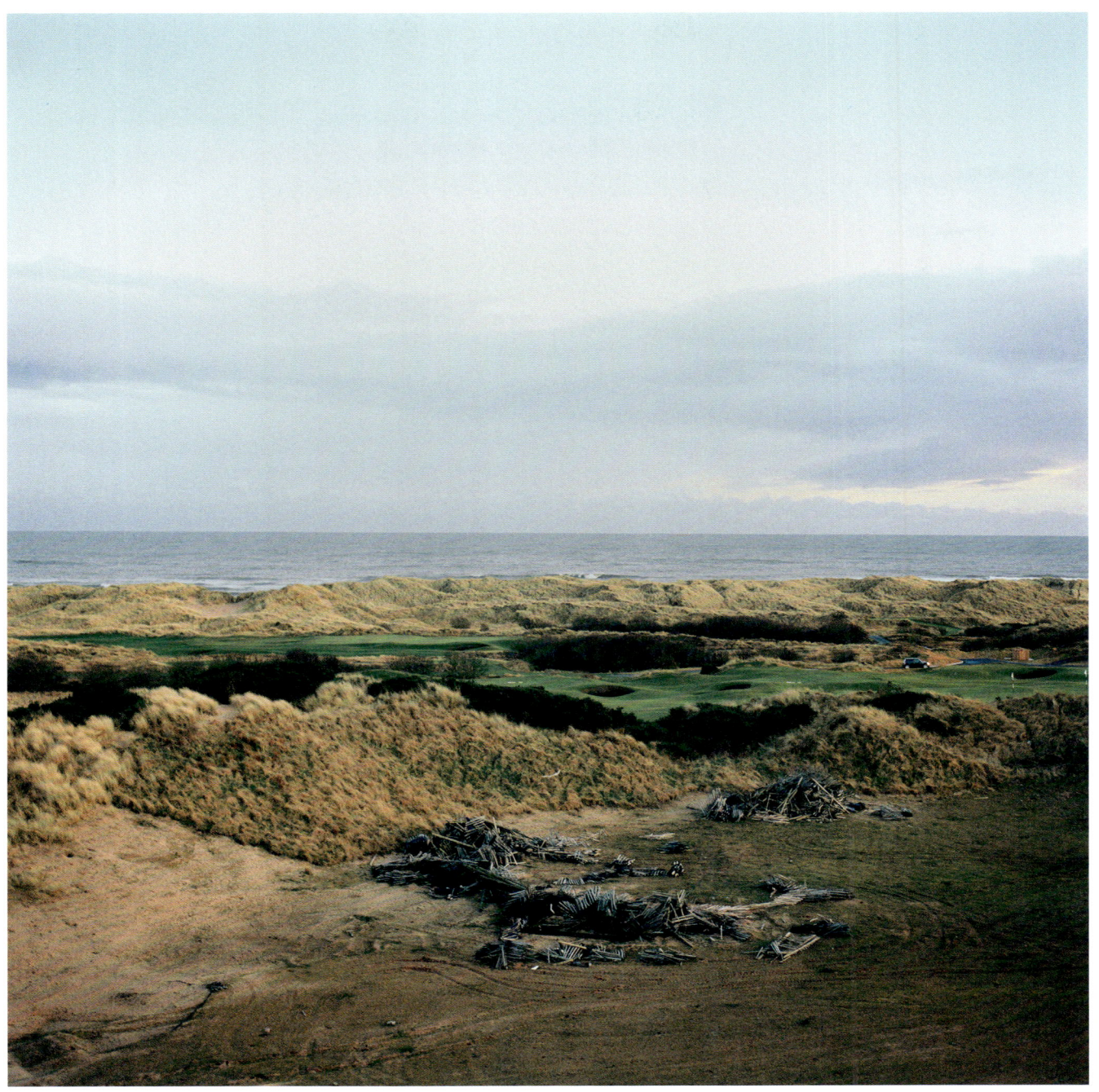

This would have been the view from Trump's proposed hotel. An area not visible from the golf course – but visible from Hermit Point – was used as a dumping ground for fencing, debris, and more; March 2011.

We brought up our kids here. We put our hearts and souls into the house and the garden. I feel as though I'm in with the woodwork now. We used to call it 'the land that time forgot'. We heard a rumour Donald Trump was about to buy or had bought the estate in 2005 or 2006. We thought it was a bit of a joke. At that point, all he was was this ridiculous man you saw in films or whatever. Innocent days!

We've had a few run-ins with overzealous Trump security, even being stopped when trying to get into our drive and being asked, were we on the guest list? They used to drive slowly after us while we were walking the dog.

I met Donald Trump once when the golf course first opened. The neighbours were invited, and I asked why he had put up locked gates. I think everybody says yes to him.

For a long while, the local press played a very pro-Trump role and had a close connection with Trump, as Sarah Malone, Trump Scotland's executive vice president, was married to the editor of the *Press and Journal*.

It's been very stressful for more than fifteen years. My husband Don and I were active with a petition against development. We ran a good campaign, but after Don was diagnosed with grade four glioblastoma, an aggressive form of cancer, at the start of 2009, we had to take a back seat. We had to prepare and fight and speak at meetings and comment on multiple planning applications. It's always there on your shoulder. You are always thinking, what next? Now the housing development is getting underway with more building work near my house, and that's going to be disturbing. It's just a vague feeling of having an uncomfortable neighbour, of unease, because you never know quite what's going to happen.

—Val Banks, Menie resident, 2023

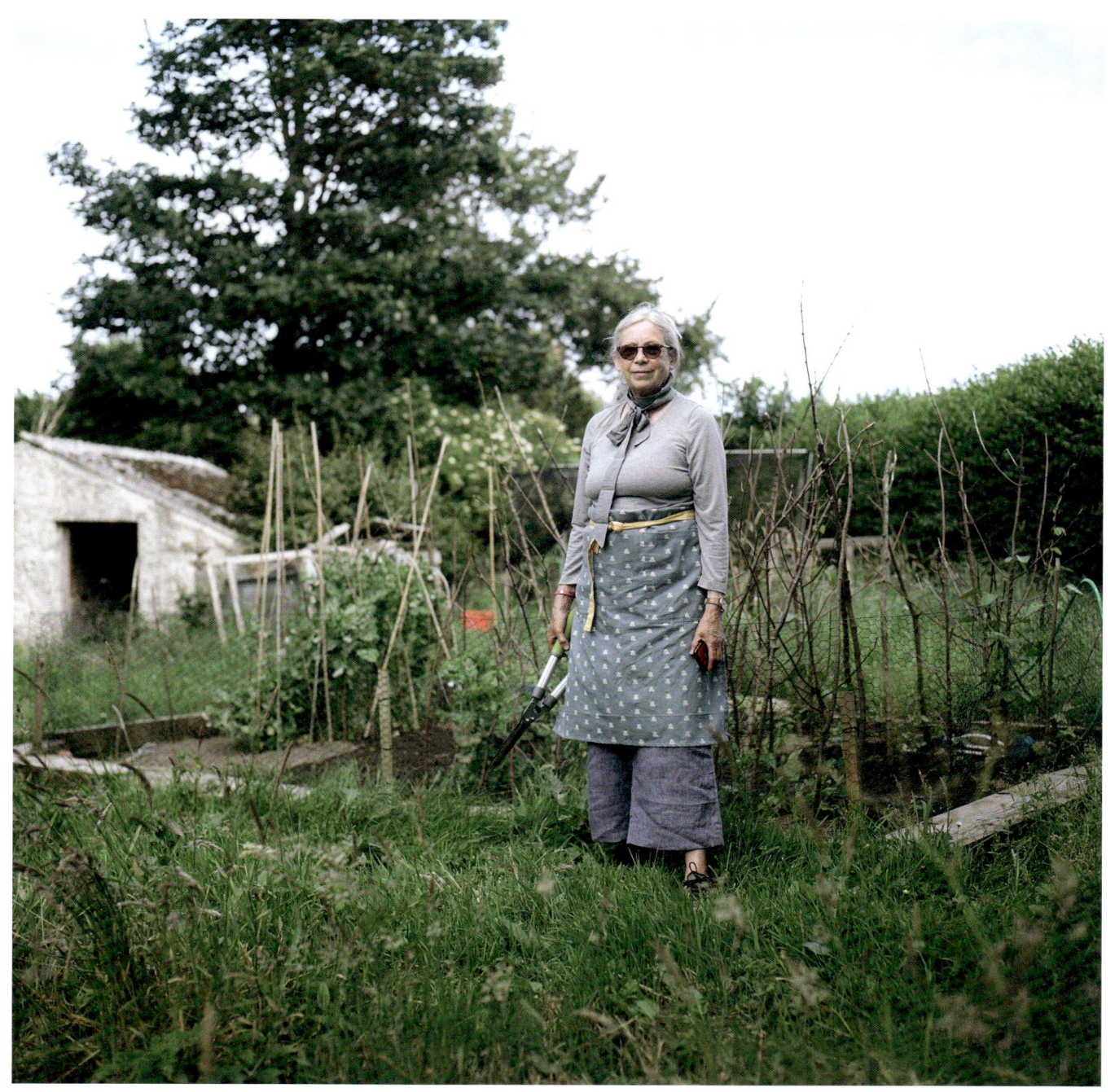

Val Banks, West Lodge, Menie, 16 July 2022.

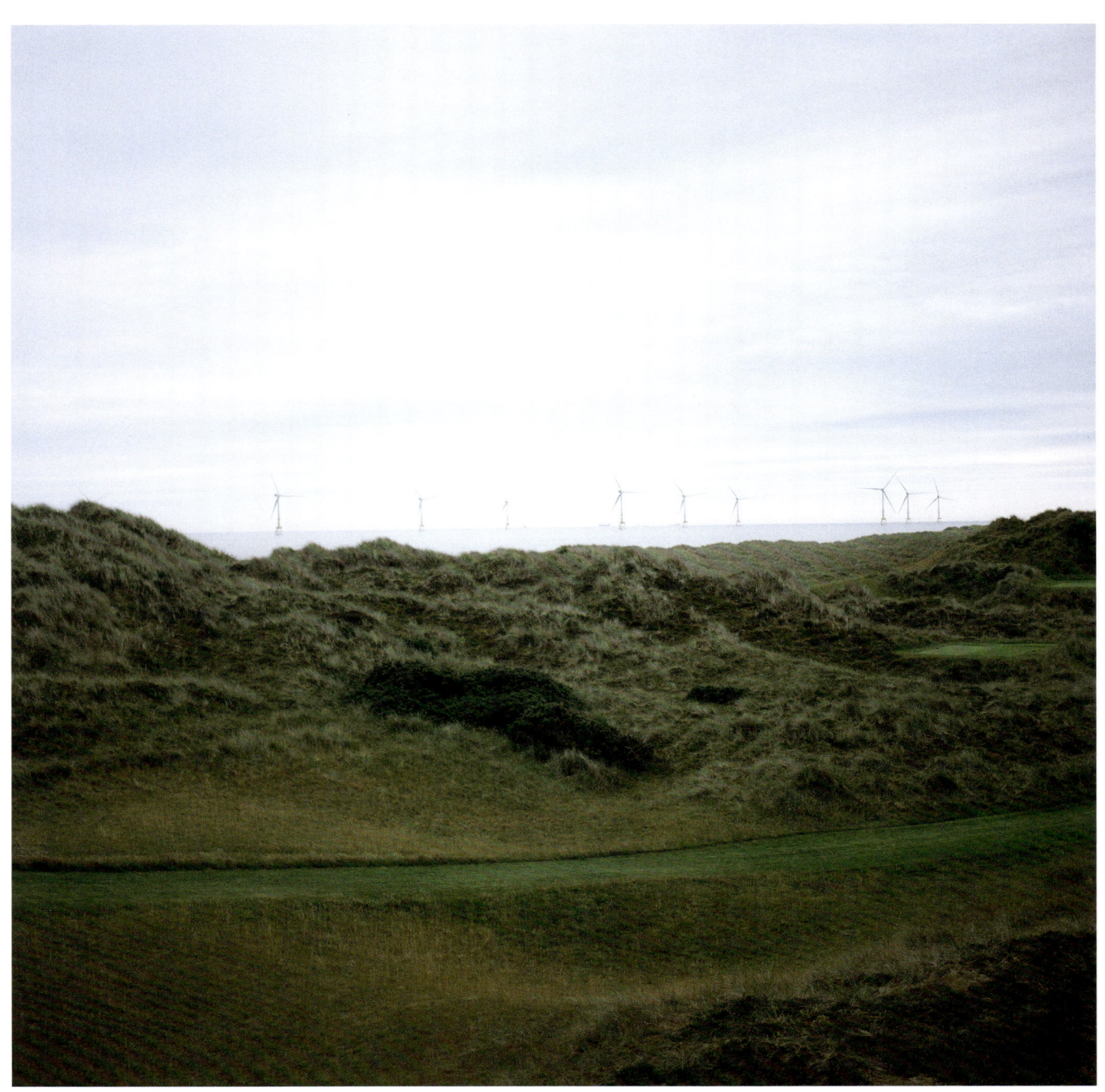

Saturday afternoon at Trump International Golf Links Scotland, July 2022.

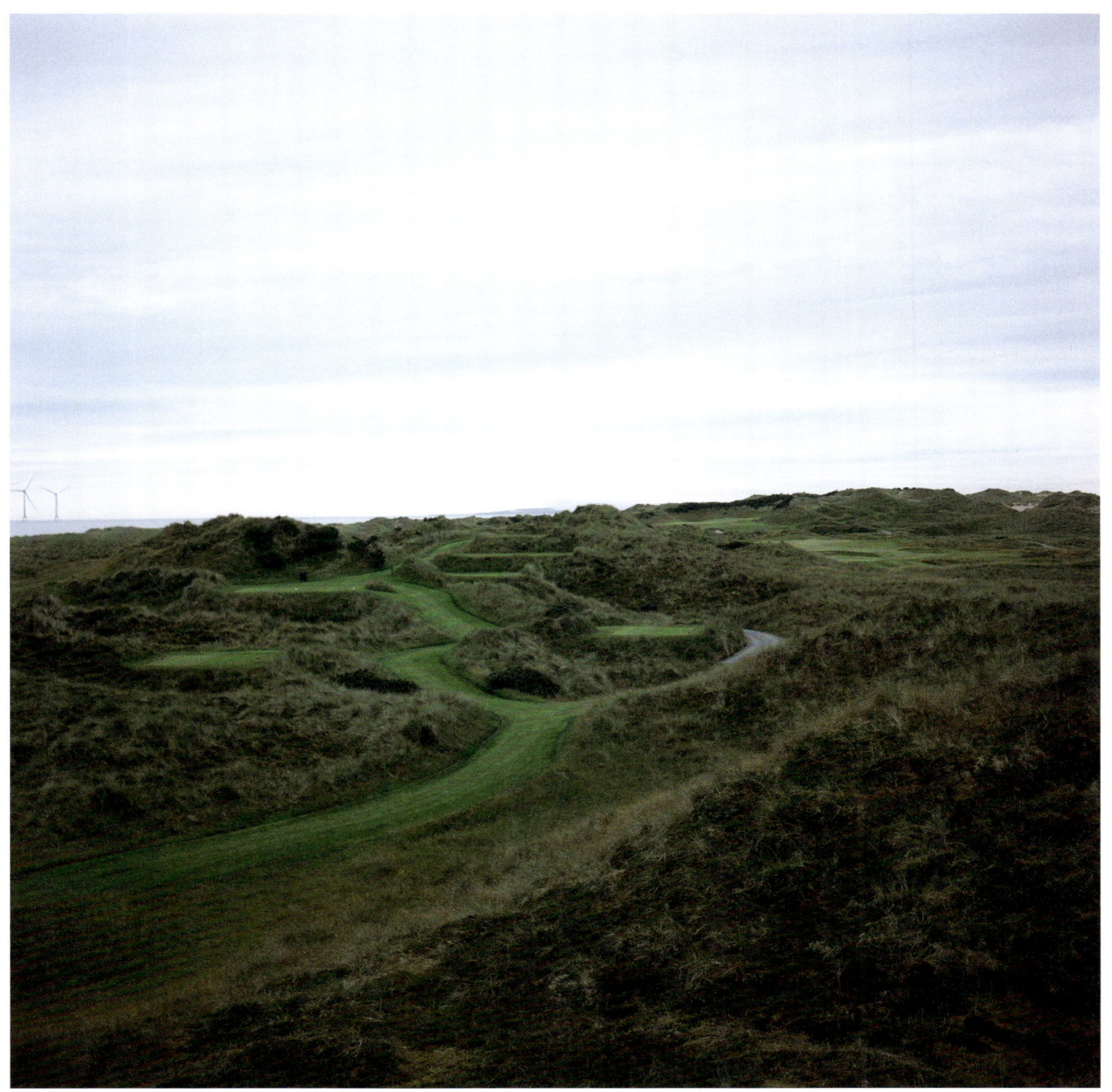

The wildness of the dynamic dune system touches the mind, body, and spirit. Trouble is, the dune system was a rare gem and once it's gone, it's gone. Nature will fight back but the SSSI accreditation is gone. Is anywhere on this planet safe? I feel very sad about what's happened here on a spiritual level. We lived so in tune with nature and fought to keep its ruggedness and wildness preserved. My late partner Mickey's punk spirit came through campaigning against the development. I think everybody should have the right to experience wild landscape, especially as modern life is taken over with technology. My fondest memories are of walks with my lovely Newfoundland through the amazing landscape. The only positive of this situation is in bringing our community together to campaign to save such a rare beauty spot from being totally commercialised.

—Kym Swindells, Menie resident, 2023

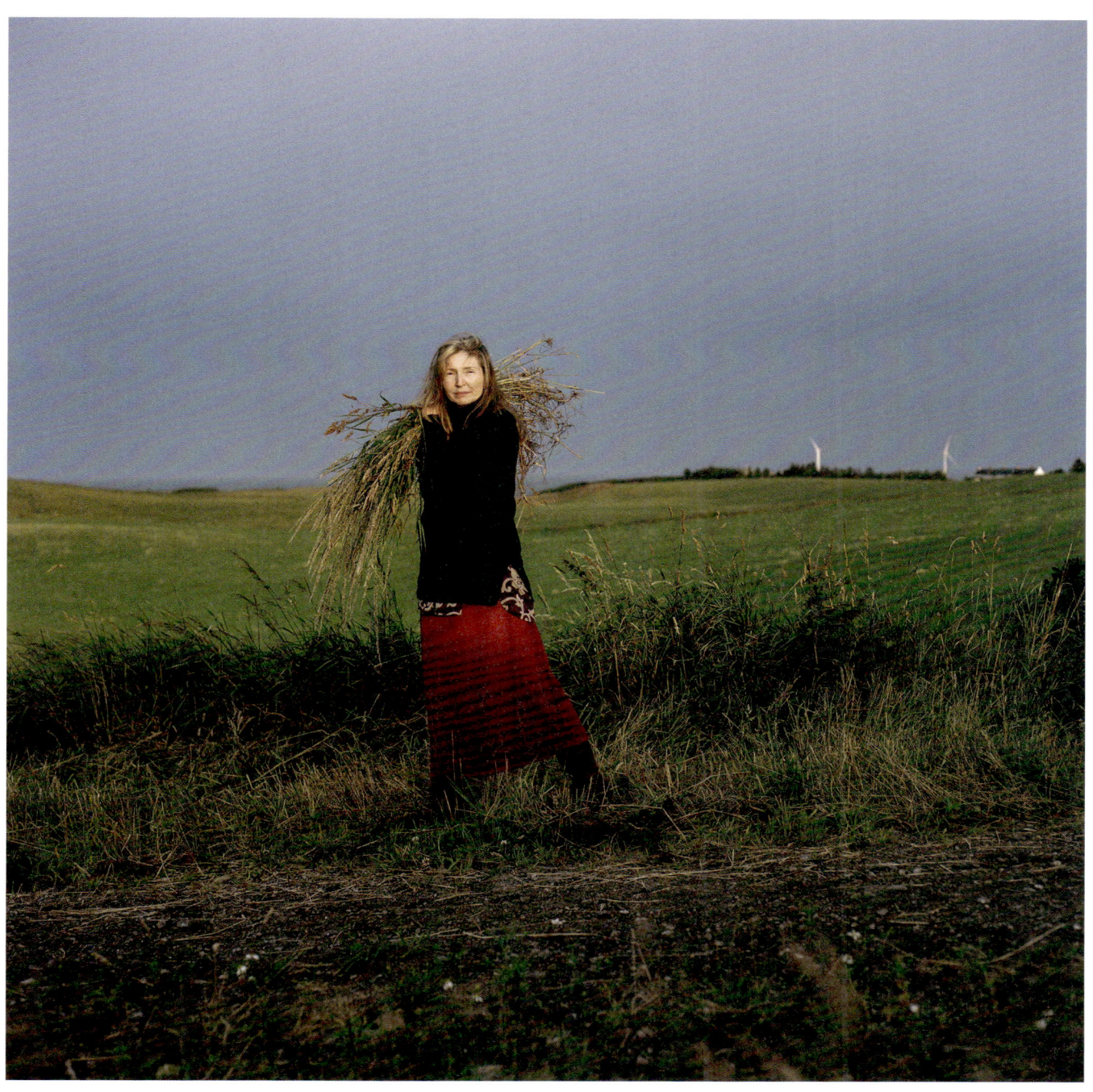

Kym Swindells, 17 July 2022.

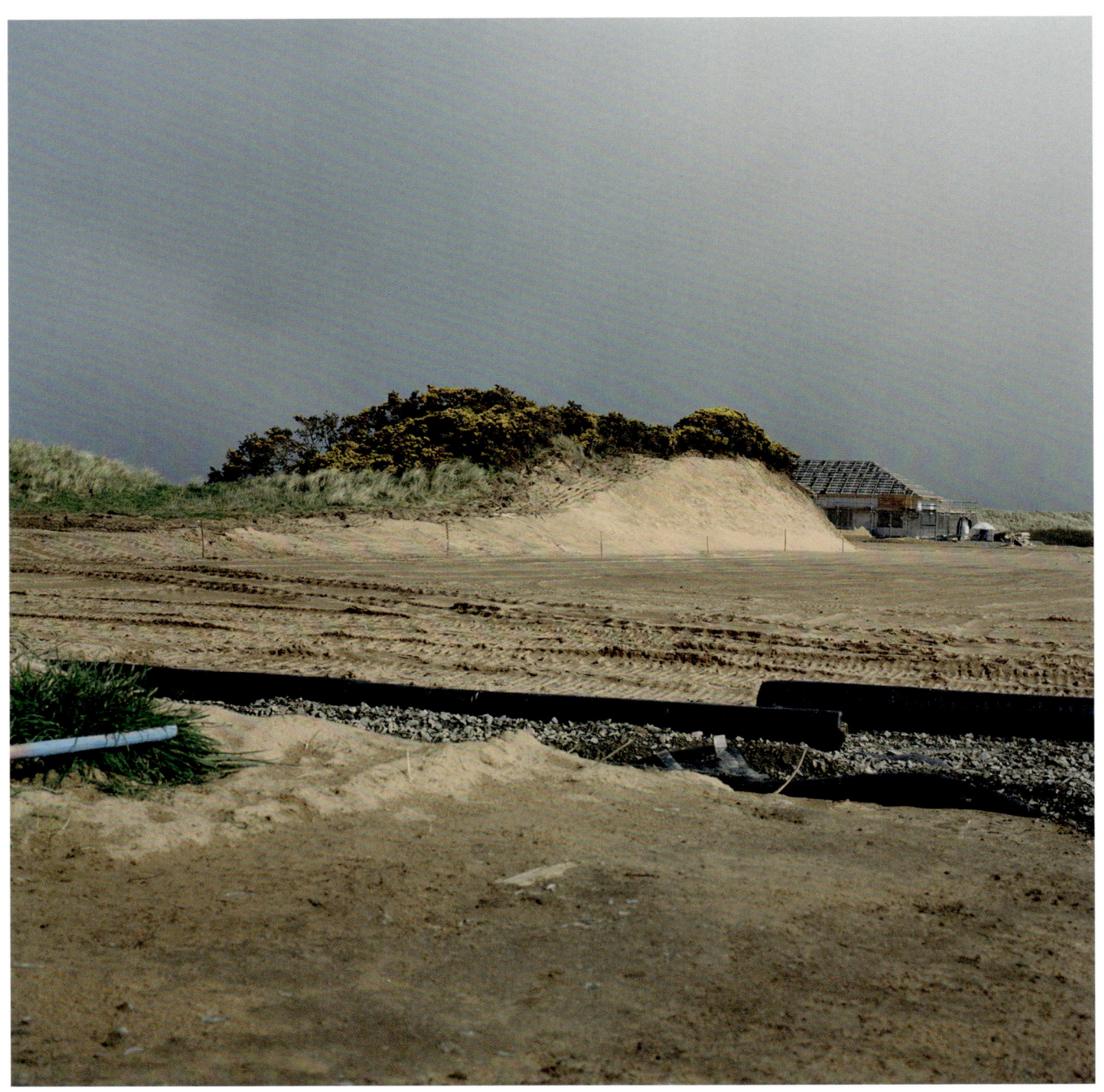

Ripped-up sand dunes destined to become Trump International Golf Links Scotland's car park, with temporary clubhouse construction visible behind a dune. This area is at the edge of Leyton Cottage, the formerly remote home of Susan and John Munro; February 2011.

Nature fights back,
as sand flies from the
dunes descend on the
golf course,
January 2013.

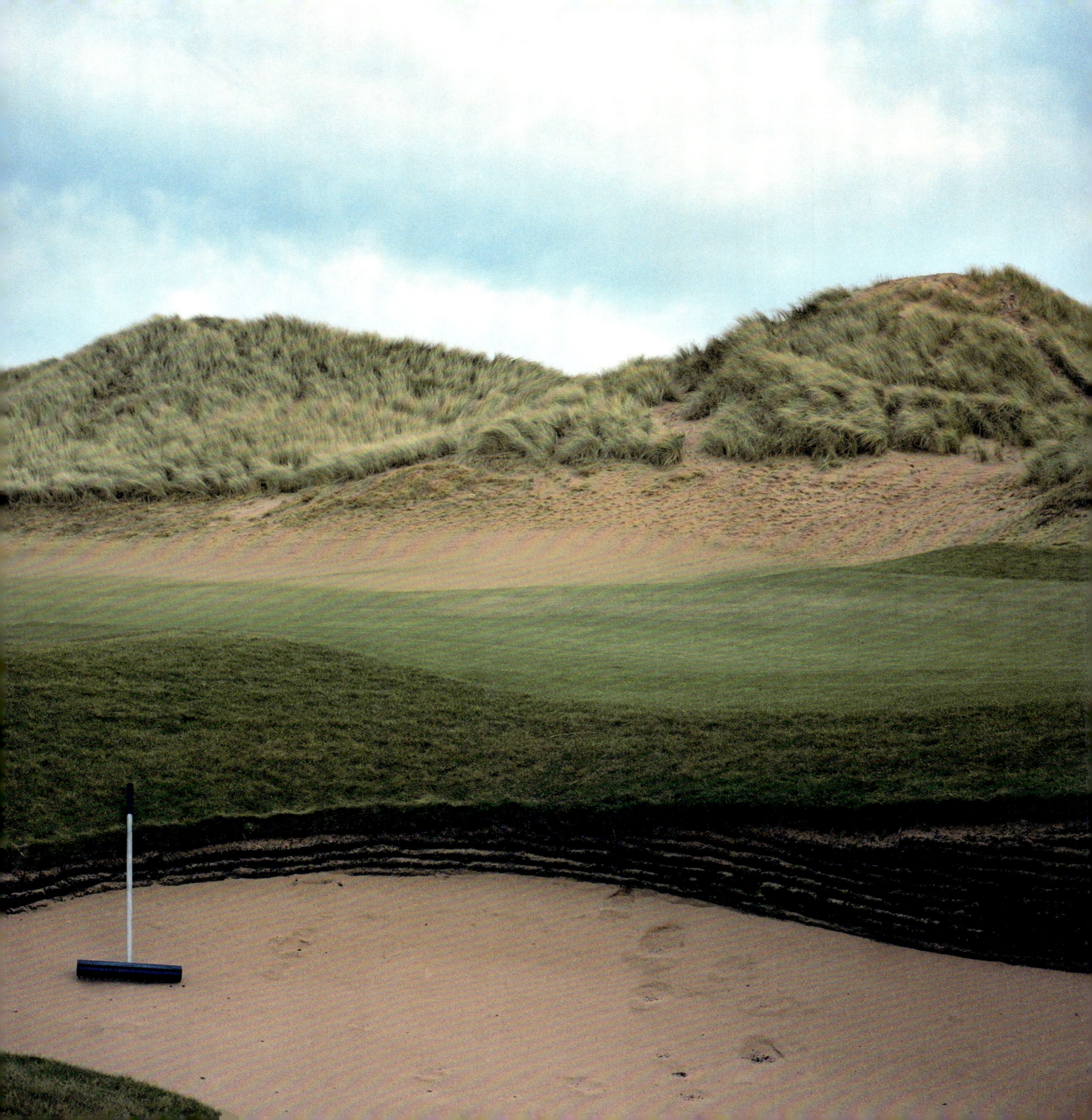

Trump said my hoose was a pigsty when they tried for compulsory purchase orders. Well, it's my pigsty. I said, it's my home and they won't put me out of it. There's been nae positives. He's ruined the dunes; he's just ruined everything. Everything he touches, he ruins. He's scared away all the wildlife apart from deer – that's aboot all ye see doon here now. Afore Trump you'd see otters; you name it, they used to be here. He maybe thinks he could make things bonnier, but there's nithing bonnier than nature.

They couldn't put a clown in charge of America, surely? But they did! I went over there, but they wouldn't listen to me. He lost his seat. He thinks he was cheated out of it. I hope he disnae get back in again because if he dis, he'll just take America tae its knees.

He blocked off my access to the beach so I couldn't do my salmon fishing, and the police took his side. I would say the worst thing he did was try for compulsory purchase and blocking my access to the fishing, because he knew I loved doing the salmon fishing, and that was the only way he could get at me, because he couldnae build bunds round my hoose, because I own my land and all the land around my hoose.

In 2010, they dug up all my well pipes, supplied by a spring. Some days the water was black, but I couldn't understand why. For five years, we drunk this water, and it was poisonous. So one day I'd had enough. I went up to see what was wrong with the well and I found oot it was burst a pipe. They denied causing the damage, so I went up with my own mini digger, dug up their road, fixed the pipe, put the road back, and it's been perfect ever since. Trump said my mother reminds him of his own mother. Well, I pity his mother. Aye. I would hope he wouldn't do that to his own mother.

—Mike Forbes, Menie resident, 2023

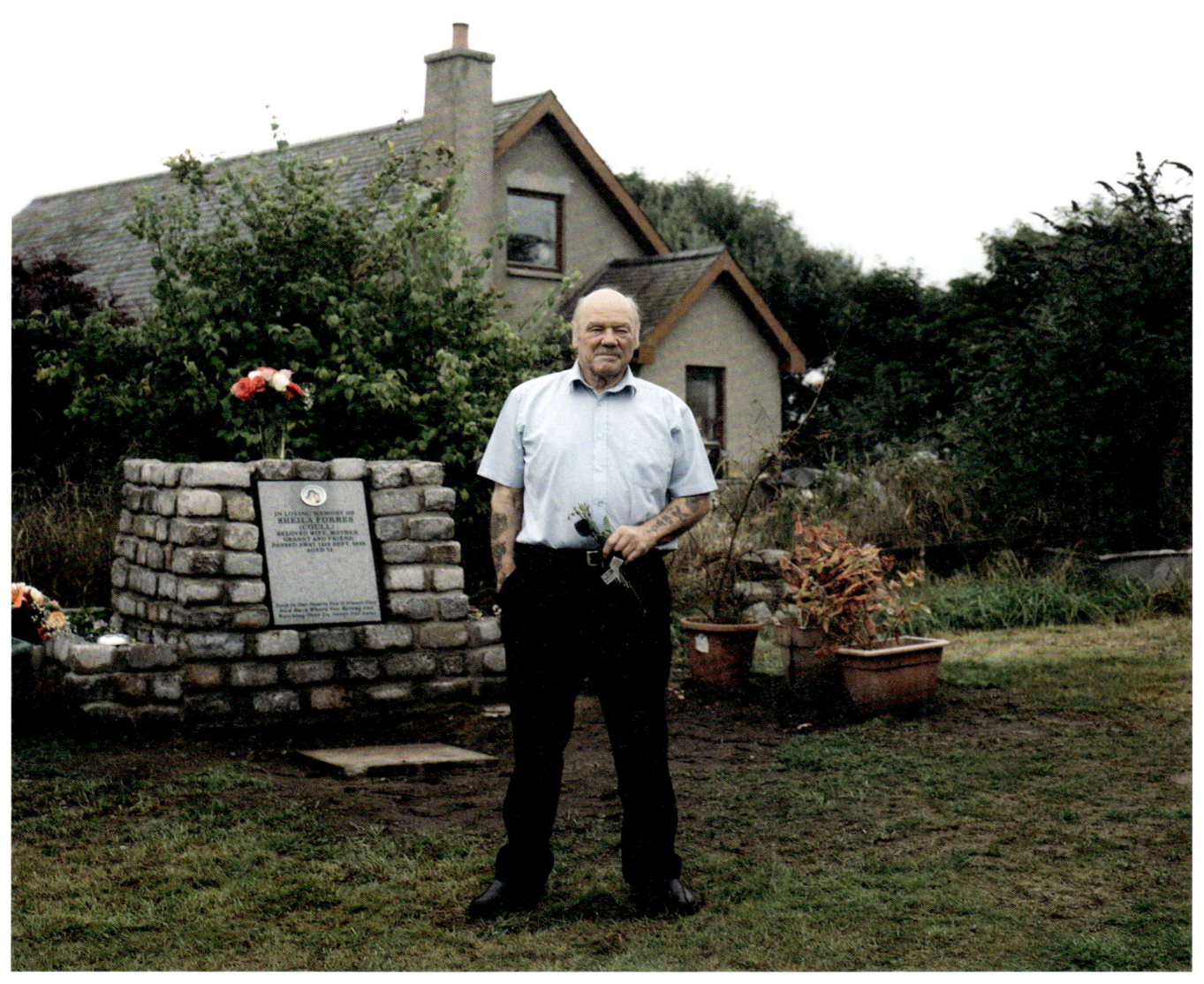

Mike Forbes, with his wife Sheila's memorial cairn on the day he buried her ashes at Mill of Menie, 11 September 2021.

Rape. View towards the existing Trump course and the dunes set to become the second course. Construction began January 2023; Summer 2011.

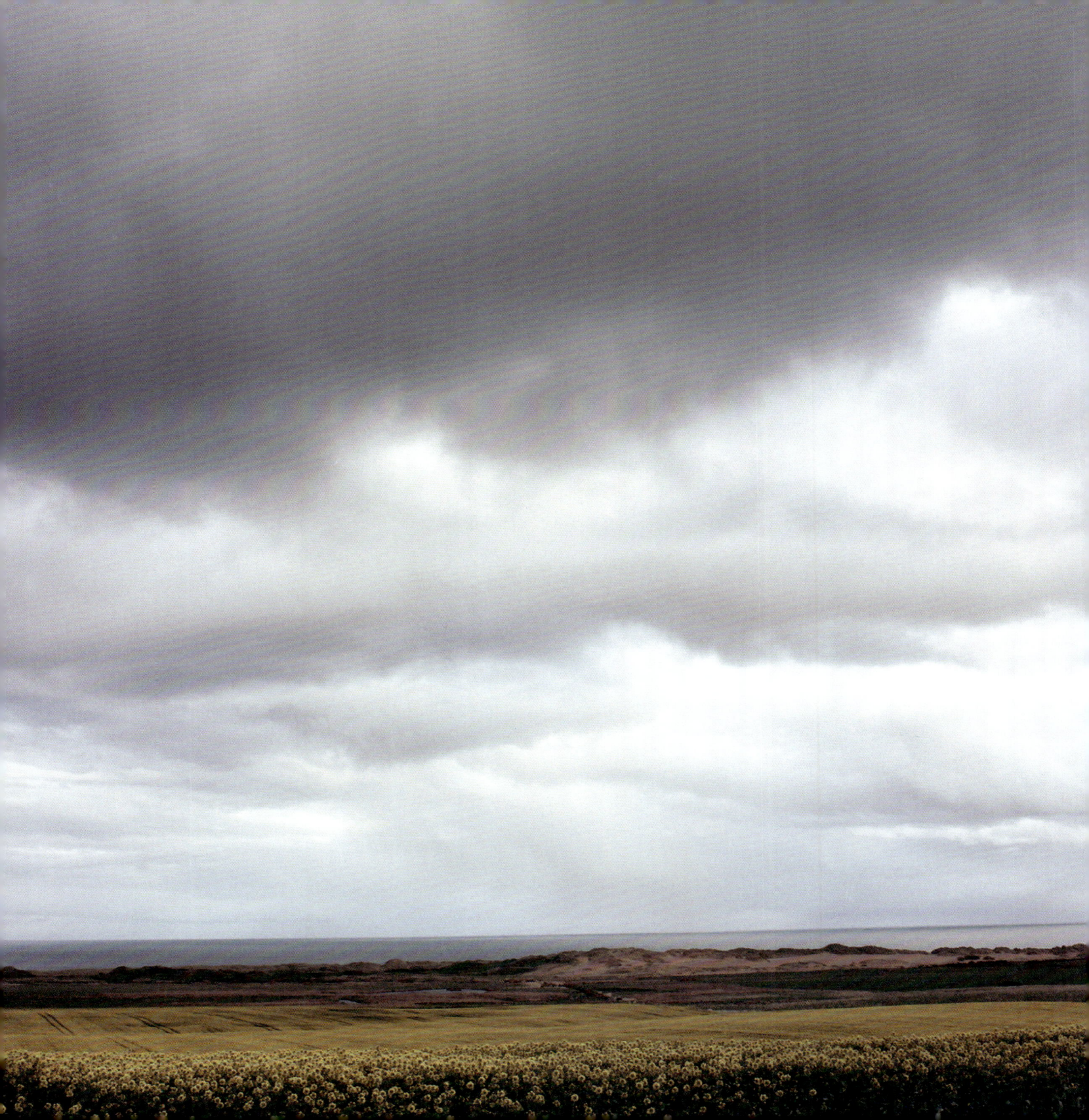

I wouldnae ken where to start. All this attention makes me feel like a celebrity and I'm nae. I'm just an ordinary person. I live in Paradise, my home in Menie, but it's feeling less like paradise these days.

The day Alicia photographed me we'd had nae water for eight days. A few days afore, Michael was washing the car and he suddenly had nae water. He came o'er and told me be careful wi the water. At first we thought it was the dry weather and the spring had gone weak. After a week one o' the boys came and said to Mike, "Have you no water?" Mike said, "Nae for a week"; they brought bottled water and said they'd get it on again. The diggers had torn up the pipe. It was three days getting it fixed and finding the broken pipe that runs into the well; it was ten days in total. Mike had to bleed it to get it into his tank; it came to mine first. It took days to get clean, as it was dirty, so we still had to use bottled water.

Well, ye canna live without water! I was carrying water for ma hens and plants from the burn. I had a barra, twa watering cans, and a paint pot wi a string. I wheeled the barra to the burn, I stood at the burnside, dippit in the paint pot, lifted it up, and poured it into the watering cans for the hens and the plants and to flush the toilet, because they were aye needing water. If they'd read the plans properly, they should have known exactly where the spring was, as it's all on the deeds.

I cannae believe the amount o' folk that's thinking o' us. A've had hundreds o' Christmas cards showing support. I aye reply if they leave an address.

—Molly Forbes, Menie resident, 2010

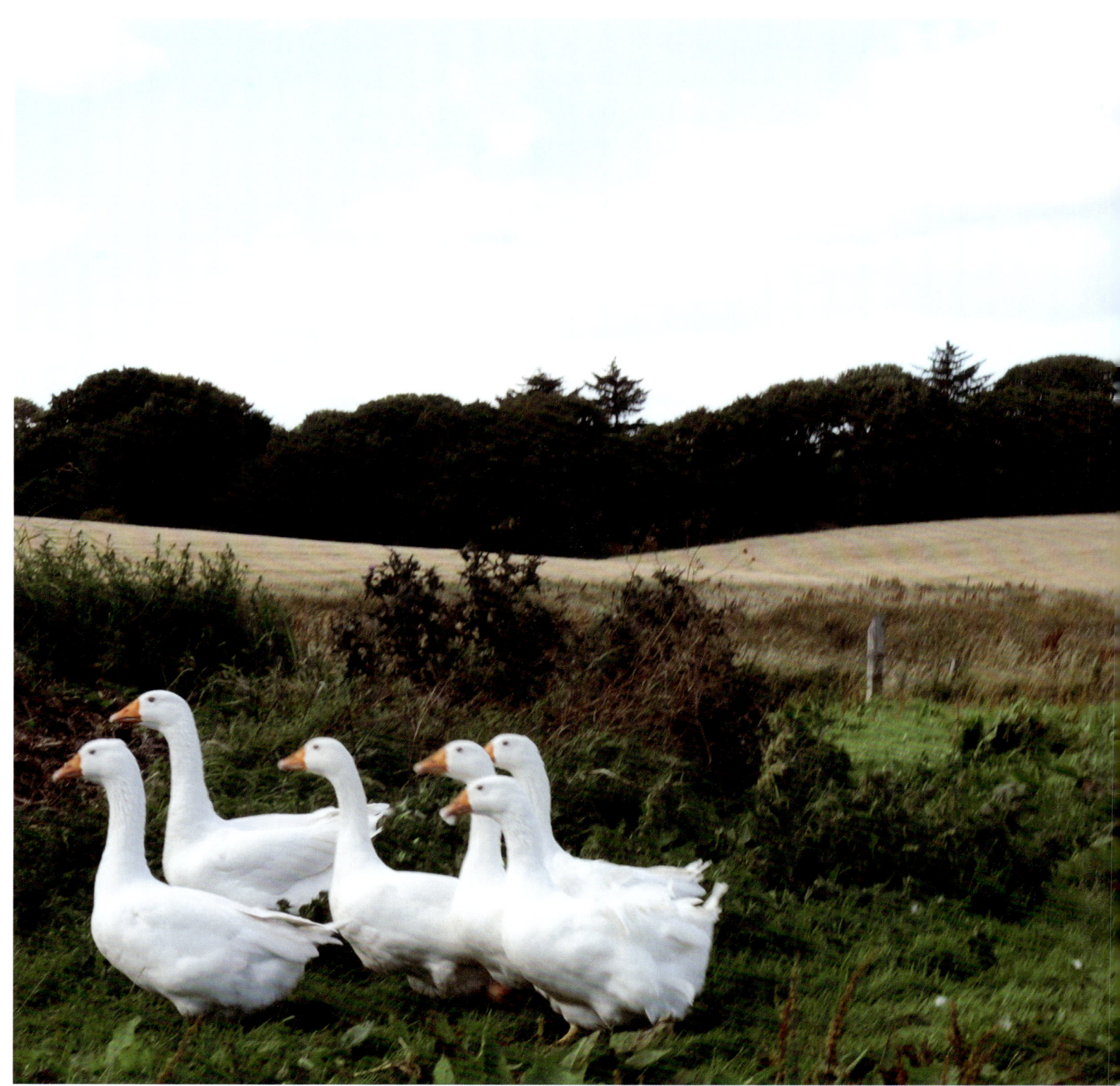

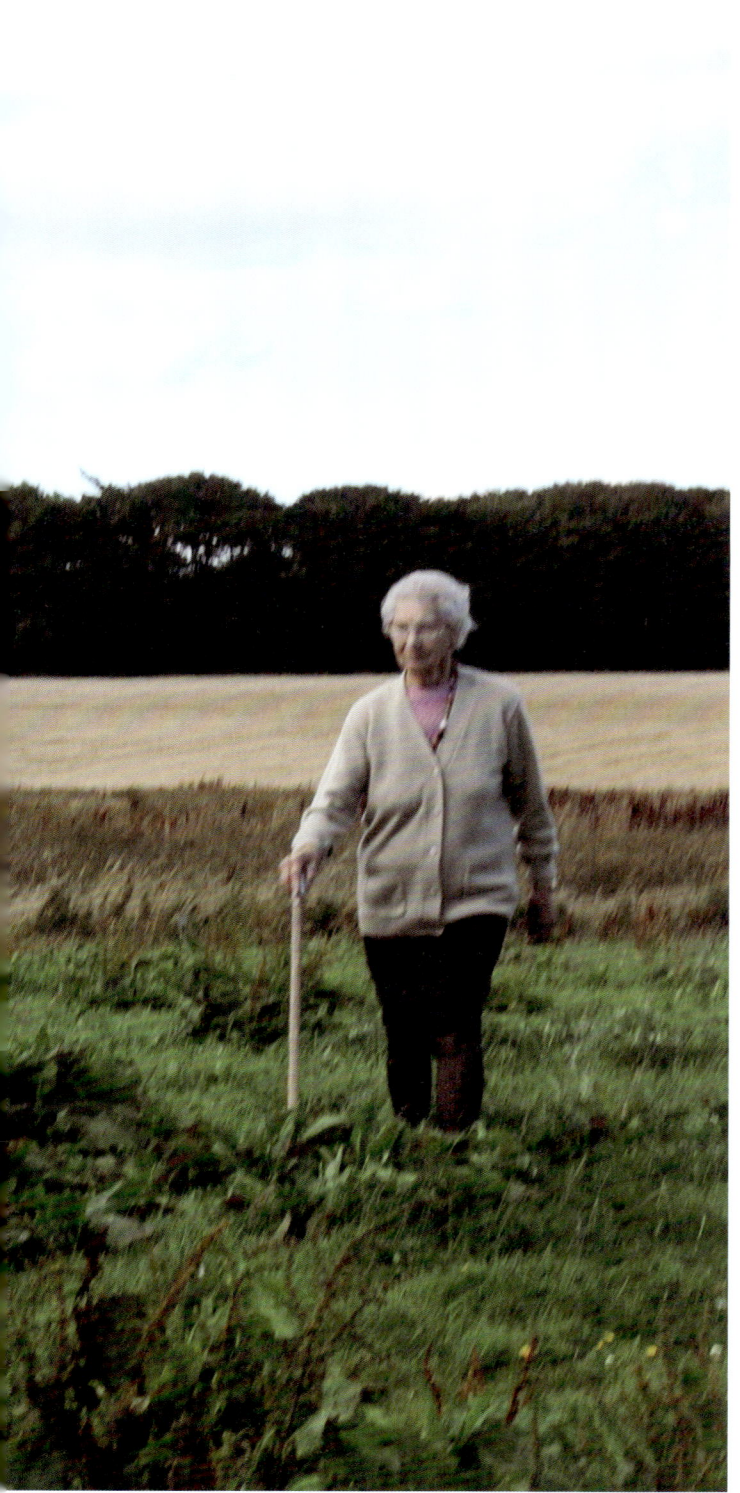

Molly Forbes,
Paradise,
21 August 2010.

These wilderness environments are our equivalent, if you like, of the
Amazon rainforests.

—Prof Jim Hansom, School of Geographical and Earth Sciences,
University of Glasgow

(Source: *You've Been Trumped*)

Nature fights back.
Golf course collapse
at Blairton Burn near
Balmedie beach as a
result of the shifting
of the dunes,
27 January 2013.

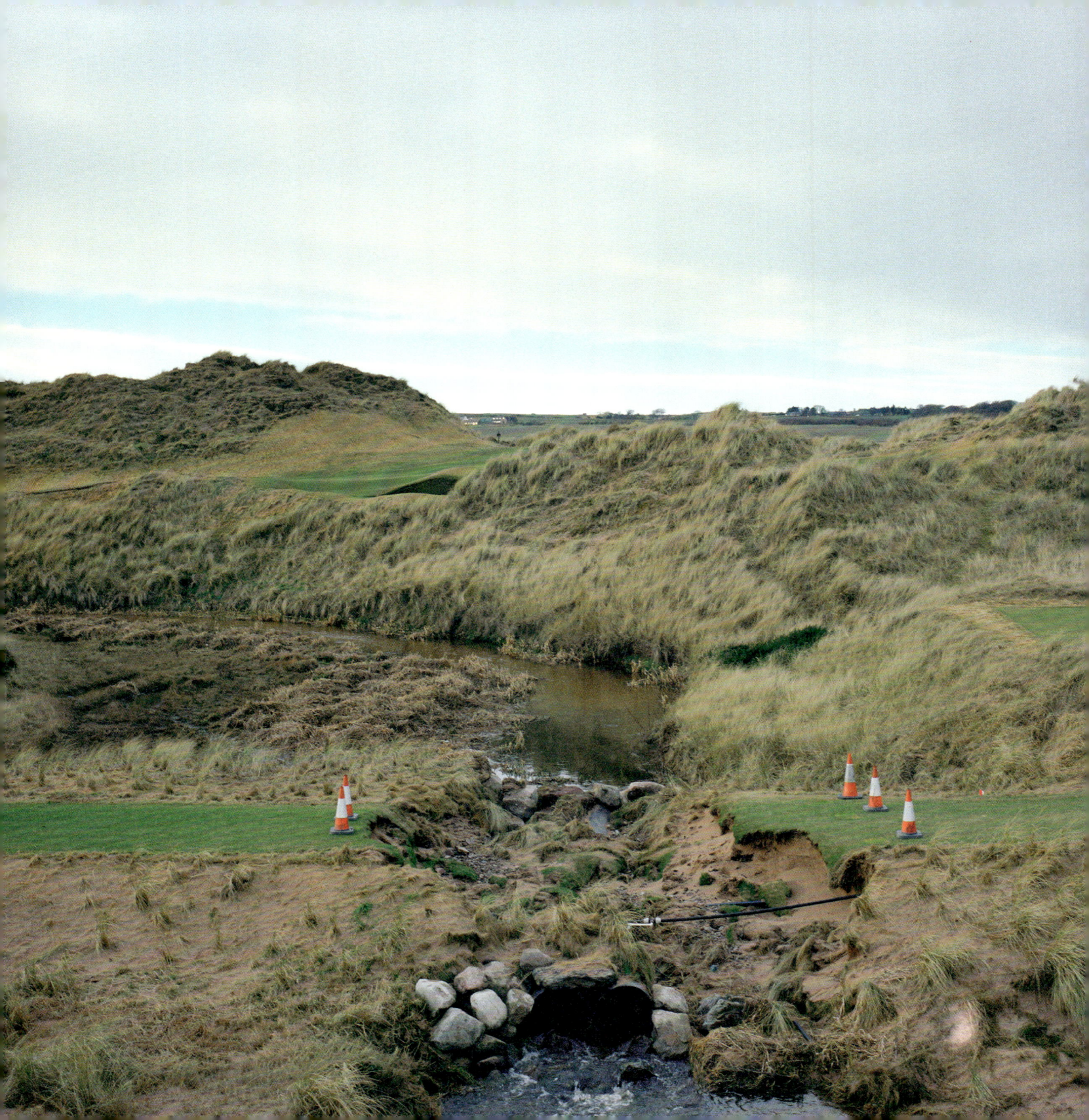

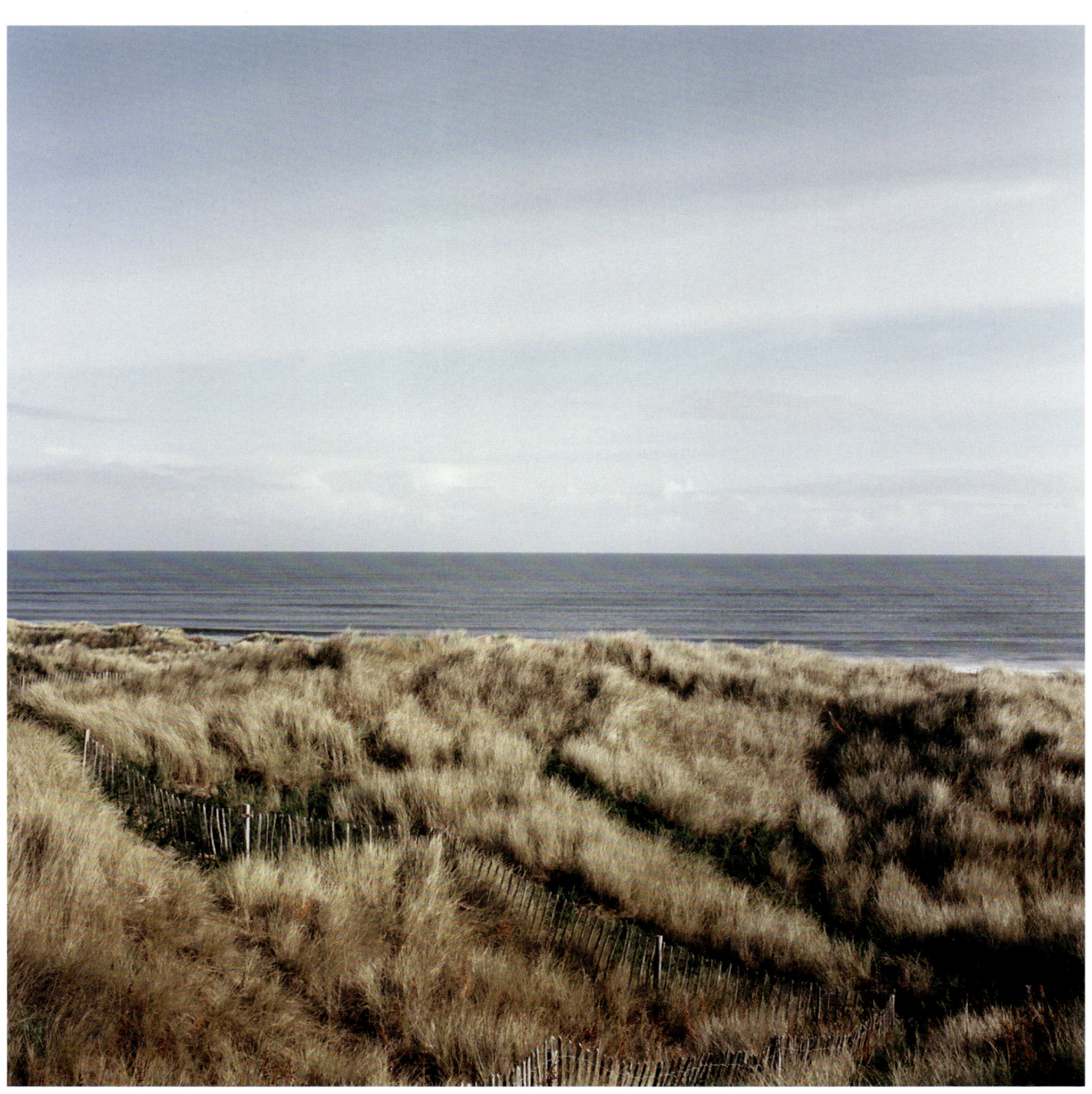

Boundary fencing and gorse planting blocking public access south of the golf course, October 2012.

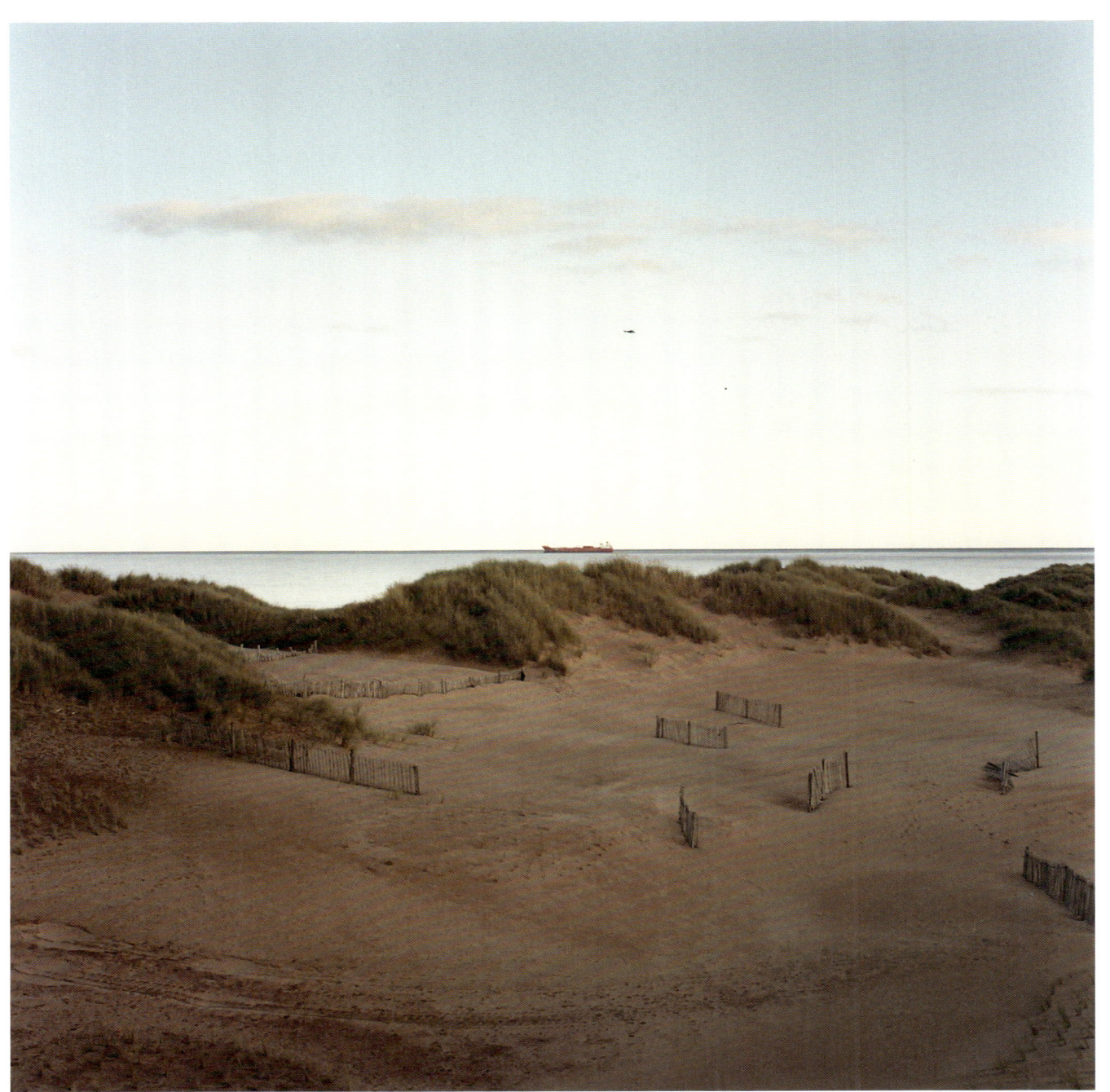

Boundary fences on Balmedie sand dunes, previously accredited as an SSSI (Site of Special Scientific Interest), July 2012.

Blairton Burn,
January 2013.

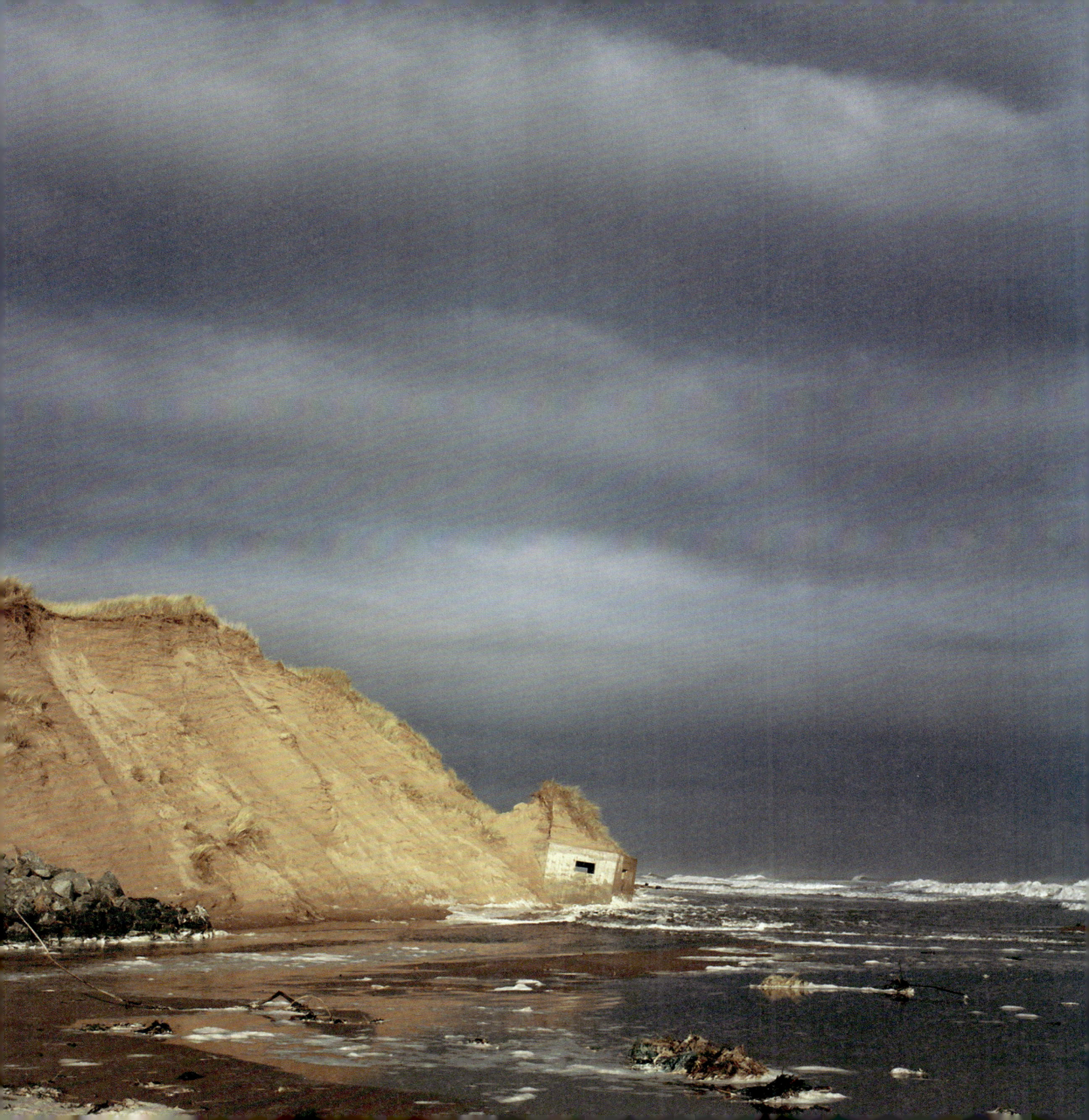

THE PORTRAITS

Interpretations by Dr Catriona McAra (CM), art historian and Lecturer in Modern and Contemporary Art History, University of Aberdeen, and Louise Pearson (LP), Curator of Photography at National Galleries of Scotland

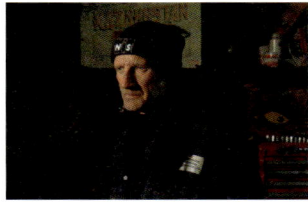 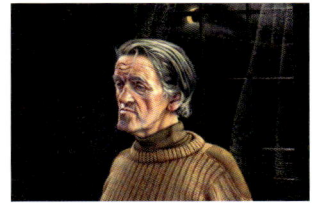

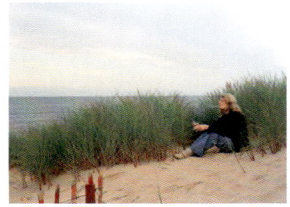 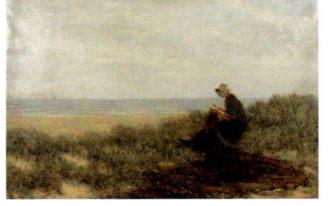

John Munro, Leyton Cottage (2010) as Erik Hoffmann's ***Nightfall: Portrait of George Mackay Brown*** **(1988)**

John finds his doppelganger in this portrait of the Scottish writer George Mackay Brown. Erik Hoffmann's expressive realist painting depicts the engrained textures of the poet's furrowed brow and uses the draught of a window at night to capture the thoughts and mood of his sitter. Bruce's portrait of John duplicates the pose but imaginatively replaces him in his natural habitat – that of the hobbyist's garage shed. In his allegorical tale 'Men and Gold and Bread', Brown writes about a peat-cutter who, after much labouring, finds a treasure chest. The peat-cutter's house goes to ruins but jewels and coins can be found embedded in the cracks. The man did not leave because he became rich – his home was his castle. (CM)

Susan Munro, Leyton Cottage (2010) as Archibald D. Reid's ***On the Bents*** **(1873)**

Equipped with a cigarette and mobile phone, Susan's portrait offers a revision of Archibald Reid's painting *On the Bents*, which depicts a woman mending some fishing nets. But the tide is high and there is tension in Bruce's version of what should be a peaceful and meditative solitude. This portrait is set closest to the dunes and presents an occupation of this site. (CM)

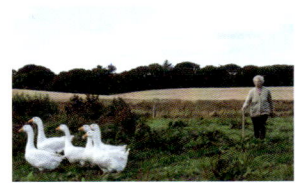 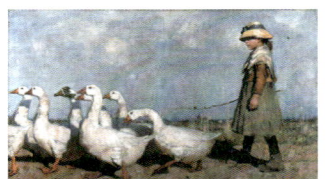 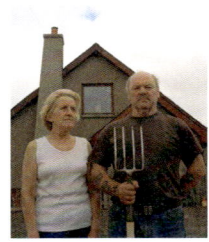 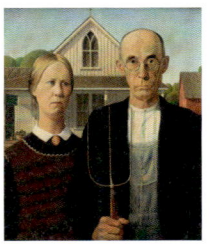

Molly Forbes, Paradise (2010) as James Guthrie's *To Pastures New* (1883)

Molly chose a Glasgow Boys painting as the starting point for her portrait. The little girl in James Guthrie's painting creates a sense of continuity – Molly, now retired, having had close family ties to this area all her life. The gaggle of geese is also fitting for her own brood of livestock who live around Paradise, Molly's semi-mobile home. Even getting water for them is now a challenge, no thanks to the construction site on her doorstep. (CM)

Mike and Sheila Forbes, Mill of Menie (2010) as Grant Wood's *American Gothic* (1930)

Molly's son Mike and his wife Sheila's confrontational portrait breaks the mould. In contrast to the others in this series, theirs 'trips up Trump' on his home ground through an appropriation of an oft-parodied American painting in an American collection. This choice offers a witty riposte to the personal remarks made about the Forbes family property. In *American Gothic*, Grant Wood imaginatively depicts an austere colonial couple posed outside their Gothic Revival house. The artist seems to challenge the idyllic scenes of rural agriculture of the period by introducing a more sombre social commentary. Bruce's portrait of Mike and Sheila is also importantly set outside their home, Mill of Menie – the one they will not, and should not, ever be forced to leave. (CM)

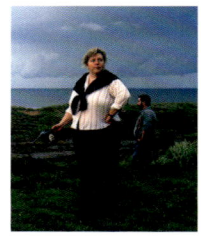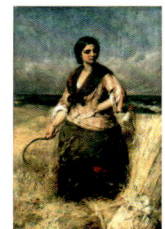

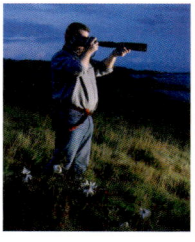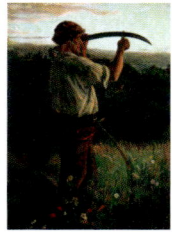

Moira Milne, Hermit Point (2010) as Thomas Faed's *The Reaper* (1863)

Replicating the details of clothing and skyline in Thomas Faed's *The Reaper* almost exactly, Moira playfully exchanges the sickle for a watering can. The choice of trousers rather than skirt also adds a modern twist to Faed's composition. In both, the stance is proud, verging on the defiant; hand on hip, this is her land and you do not mess with this woman. (CM)

David Milne, Hermit Point (2010) as Arthur Hughes' *The Mower* (1865)

Moira's husband, David, likewise substitutes the scythe accoutrement depicted in Arthur Hughes' *The Mower* for a telephoto lens. However, the tartan braces on his trousers and flowers at his feet remain consistent with the original painting. David's prop is a cunning visual commentary for the situation at hand – the view from his house is now obscured by Trump's building site. (CM)

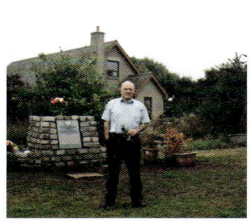
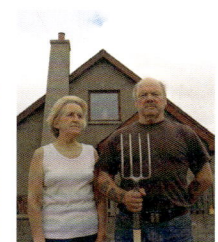
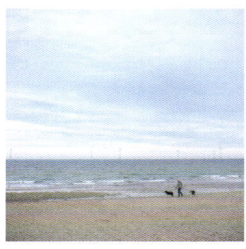
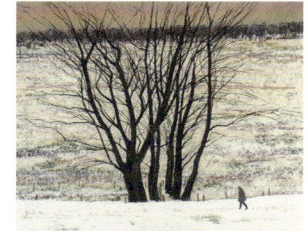

Mike Forbes with Sheila's cairn the day he lowered her ashes (2021) with Mike and Sheila Forbes, Mill of Menie (2010)

In this photograph Alicia Bruce revisits an earlier portrait which cast Mike and Sheila Forbes as Grant Wood's *American Gothic*. The poignance of this image lies in what has changed and what hasn't. Mike still stands in front of his home, testament to over a decade of resilience. But instead of standing beside his wife, he stands alongside her cairn. It is a portrait of strength – of a marriage, of the bond the photographer has to this family, and of a woman who stood for and protected what she held dear. (LP)

Sue Edwards, Balmedie beach (2022) as Victoria Crowe's *Large Tree Group* **(1975)**

In this photograph, Sue takes the place of shepherd Jenny Armstrong in Victoria Crowe's contemplative painting. For fifteen years, Crowe painted her friend and neighbour Jenny at work in the Borders, documenting her changing relationship with the landscape. Both women cut a solitary, defiant figure. Echoing the composition of the original painting, here snow is replaced by sand and trees are substituted for the Aberdeen Bay wind turbines which Trump opposed. (LP)

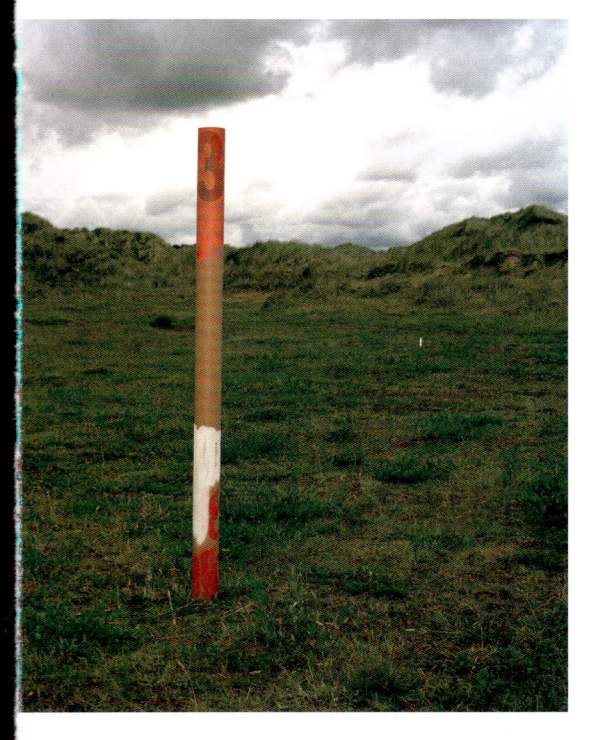 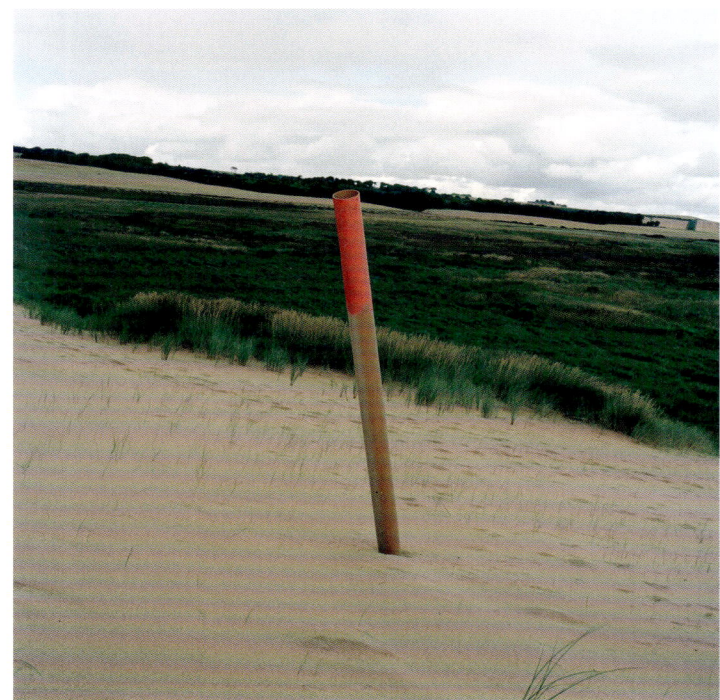 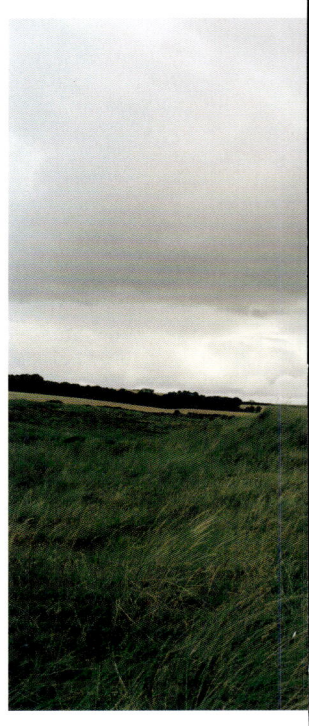

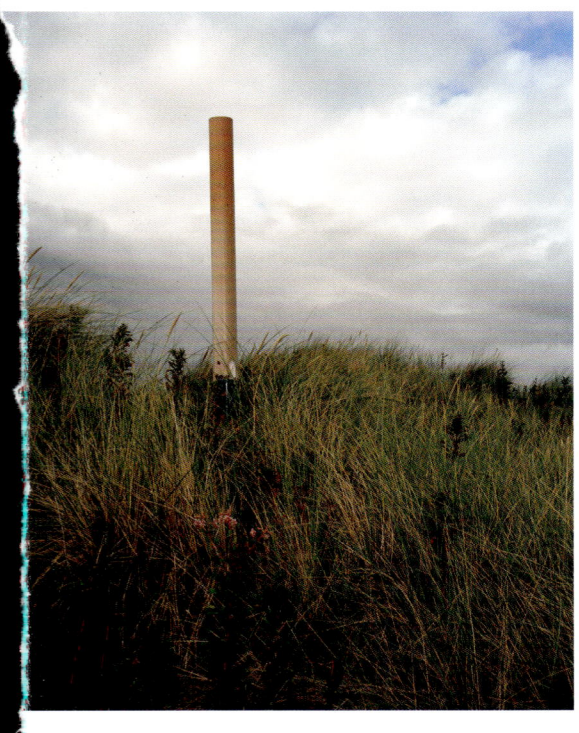 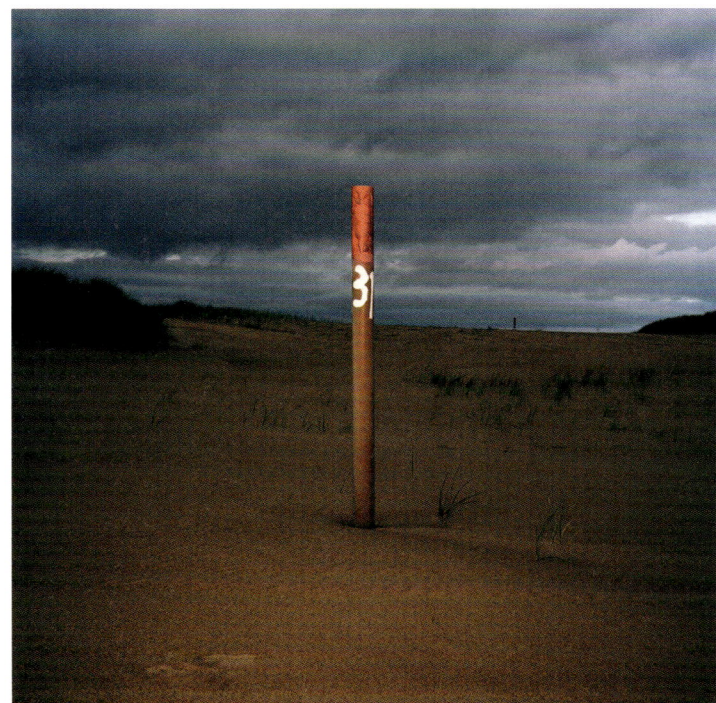 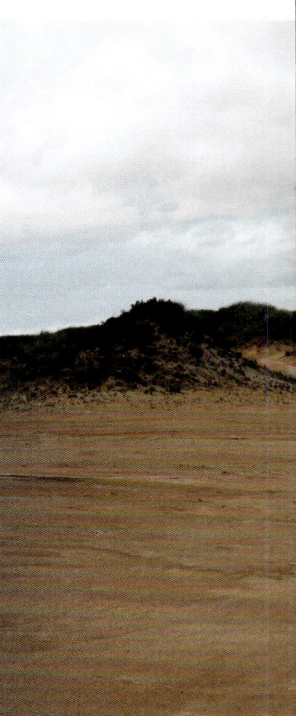

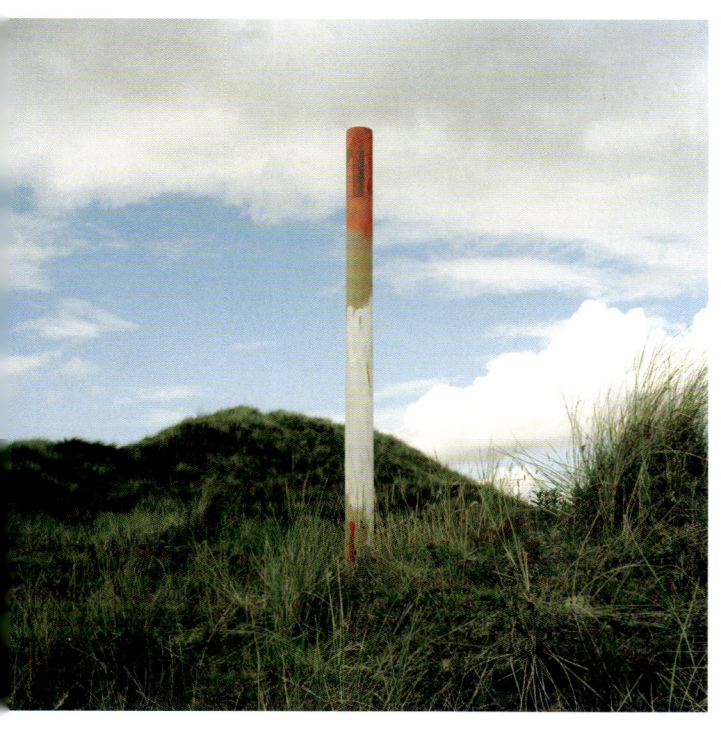
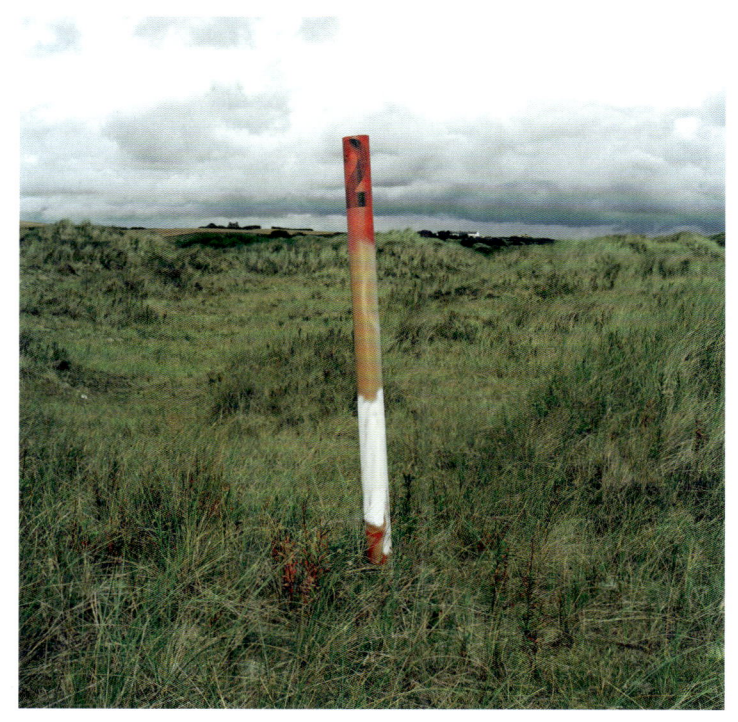

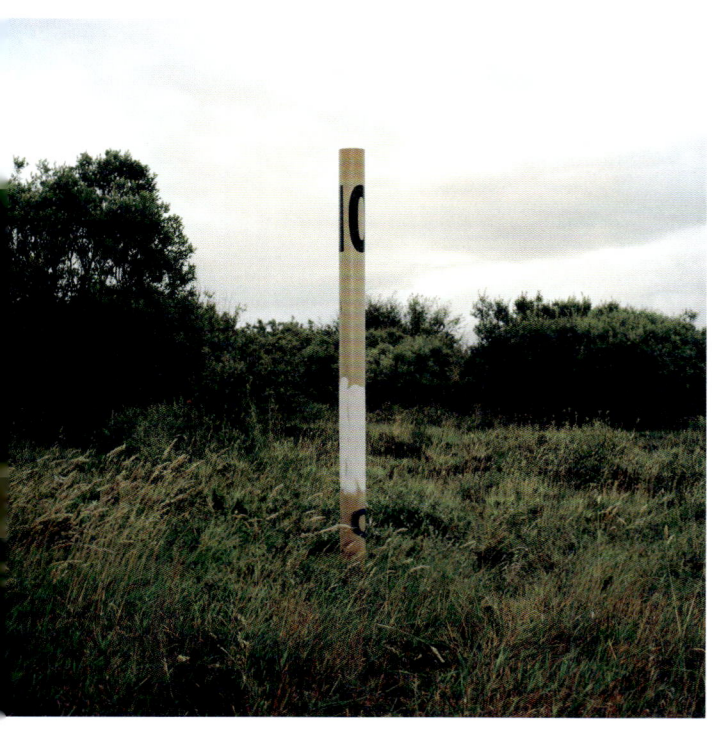
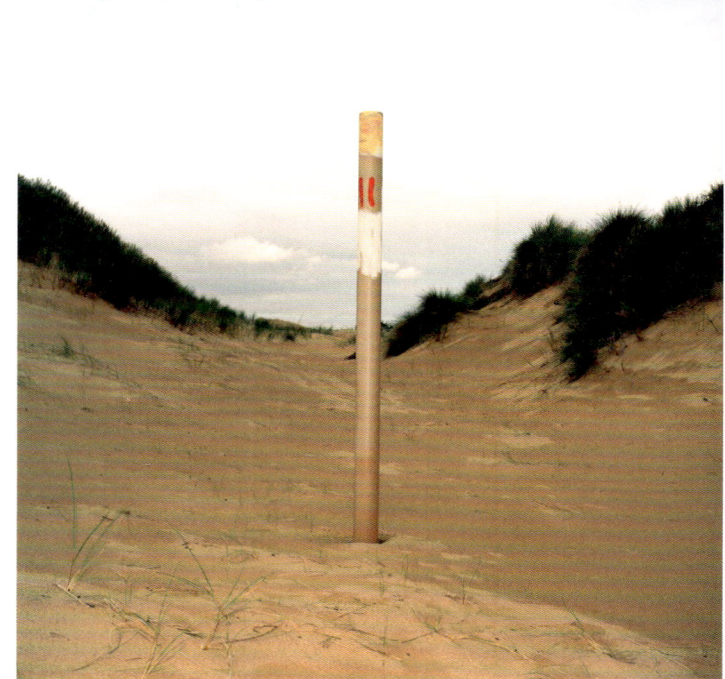
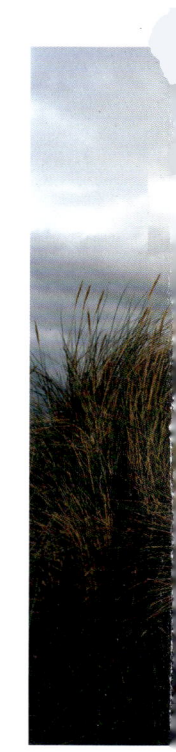

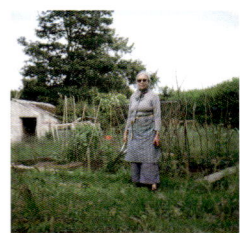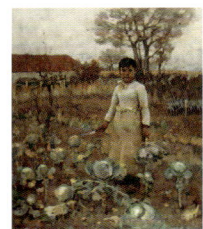

Val Banks, Menie Lodge Cottage (2022) as Sir James Guthrie's *A Hind's Daughter* (1883)

Val is rooted in her land. Like the young girl in Guthrie's painting, she has just straightened up from tending her garden, tool (and mobile phone) in hand. She continues to plan for the future and prepare for the season ahead despite construction work creeping closer to her home. Val is Trump's closest neighbour, her peaceful rural lifestyle under renewed threat as he seeks to build housing nearby. (LP)

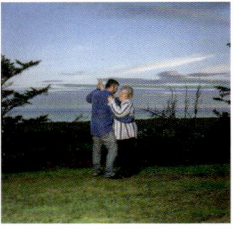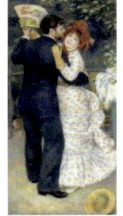

David and Moira Milne, Hermit Point (2022) as Auguste Renoir's *Dance in the Country* (1883)

At first glance, David and Moira embody the spirit of Renoir's joyful painting. They are a couple enjoying an intimate moment as the light fades over an idyllic rural scene. But when we look closer, Trump International is lurking in the dusk – its presence threatening their home and putting a strain on their relationship. Suddenly the scene seems darker, the title ominous, as we wait to see if the couple can outstep Trump's next move. (LP)

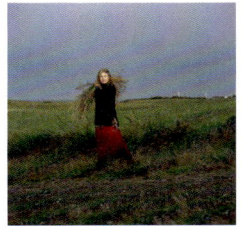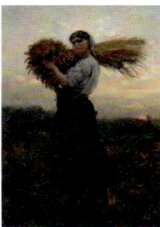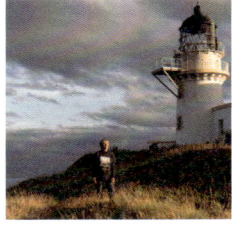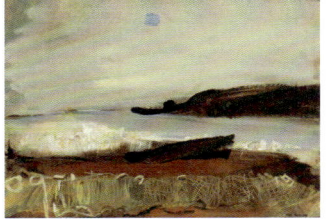

Kym Swindells, Hatterseat (2022) as Jules Breton's *The Gleaner* **(1875)**

Breton's portrait has a quiet confidence. The subject is comfortable in her own skin and is at home in the landscape around her. Meeting her defiant gaze, it is hard to imagine her anywhere else. Kym has that same sense of belonging – feet firmly planted on her land, gaze direct. Over a decade since Trump appeared on the horizon, Kym and her neighbours show no signs of leaving. (LP).

Rohan Beyts, Todhead Lighthouse (2022) as Joan Eardley RSA's *Salmon Nets on the Shore*

Campaigner and environmentalist Rohan stands by a lighthouse which overlooks the Aberdeenshire coastline that inspired Joan Eardley. From her high viewpoint she contemplates how the coastline has changed. The wild beauty that captivated Eardley remains unspoiled and unchanged whilst Rohan's beloved dunes and friends further north in Menie have been disrupted by the arrival of Trump International. (LP)

Posts. From the series *Menie: Before Trump International Golf Links Scotland*, a typology produced using a developers' map of the area.

"Photographs of the dunes, taken between 1 pm and 10 pm one day in August 2010. They depict a scene of natural beauty with its lights going out. Playing on ordnance surveys, Bruce mapped this coastal terrain which faced imminent destruction, 'Trumped' over by the proposed leisure complex. The posts are evidence of the encroaching commerce that has now swamped the area. But the tides are strong and in these photographs many of the posts are already beginning to bend as metaphors of surrender."

—Dr Catriona McAra

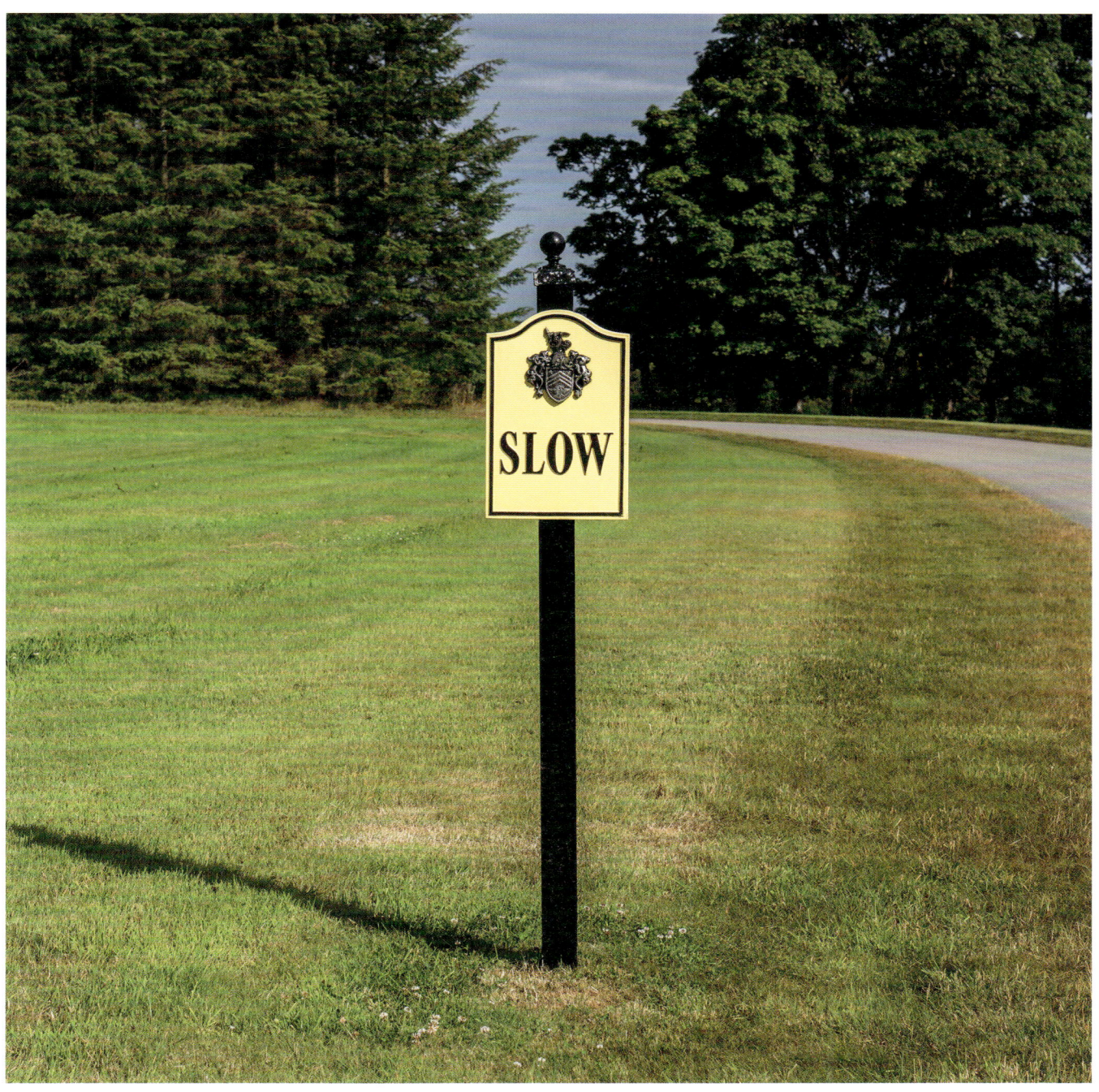

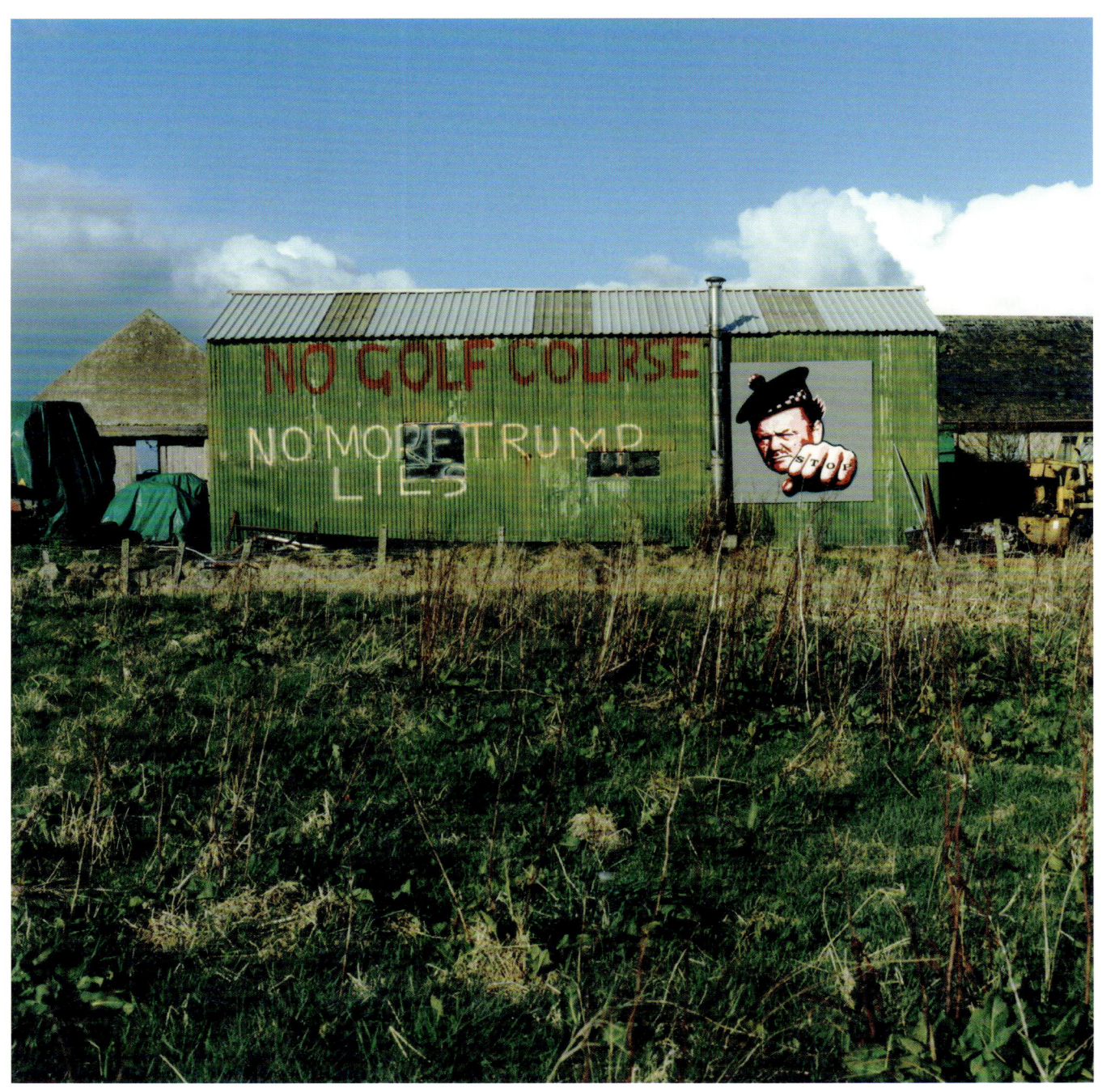

Tractor shed at Mill of Menie, the home of Mike and Sheila Forbes. Artwork of Mike by artist Michael Forbes.

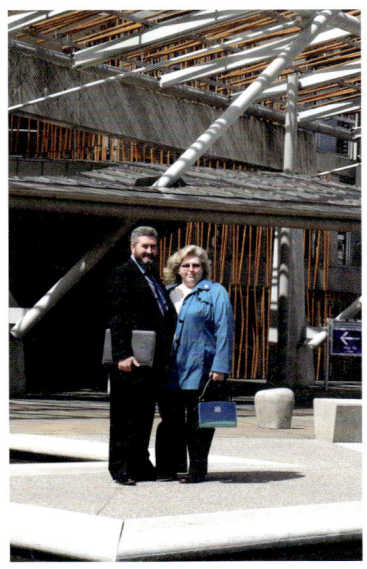

David and Moira Milne hand in a petition for a full public inquiry to the Scottish Parliament, 14 May 2013.

Despite their activism, the North East was left out in the cold – excluded from the provisions of the Crofters Act, thanks to connivance between Gladstone's government and Aberdeenshire lairds. Panicked by the arrival of Napier Commission judges to gather evidence of cruelty and arbitrary clearance in hearings from Caithness to Skye, the lairds persuaded a willing Liberal government that the resulting act should apply only in counties where evidence had been collected. Since the Commission hadn't visited Moray, Aberdeenshire, Banff, and Buchan or the rest of the North East, these were excluded from the protections of the 1886 legislation.

According to historian Ian Carter, "North-east peasants failed to realise and represent their own class interest. Capitalist farmers were allowed to present themselves as the representatives of all farmers, [but] pursued their own sectional interests."

By the time new legislation arrived in 1911, it was too late. "The north-east peasantry as a class…was dead."

The people of north-east Scotland had been cheated. Some did become tenant farmers, leasing more land than crofters would ever know. Some became very wealthy. But many left the land completely or lived and died landless, in abject poverty. By contrast, the Highland crofting counties became relatively densely populated with thousands of local people living on tiny plots of poor land. It was a tough, hand-to-mouth existence, but crofters had security, which allowed a thrawn, stable, interconnected rural society to develop across the Highlands and Islands. A society with people, memories, and expectations of something much better.

It wasn't the same in north-east Scotland. If that vast region had been included in the Crofters Act, community buyouts might be as common in and around Balmedie today as they have happily become north and west of the Great Glen Fault. As it is, parts of the North East are emptier than remote Highland glens. Estates are bought, sold, traded, and covered with trees, wind turbines, and hefty subsidies without much of a complaint raised or buyout challenge mounted. It feels normal. It feels pointless to object. Or at least it did. Until Donald J Trump bought the Menie Estate in 2006. Finally, the pretensions of a boastful, super-wealthy landowner hit the bedrock of Scotland. Its ain folk.

Local farmer Michael Forbes lived and worked on a large piece of land right in the middle of Trump's estate. Michael's land had been handed down through his family. It was his home, and he held fast, even as Trump altered the landscape all around him, earning his home a telling nickname amongst locals – 'The Bunker'.

Journalists and photographers were aggressively threatened by Trump's security guards as they approached Michael and other local residents to cover the story. The National Union of Journalists protested over the 2010 arrest and detention of documentary filmmakers Anthony Baxter and Richard Phinney, and the author of this book, Alicia Bruce, involved the police in 2012, when she was threatened for taking photographs on land belonging to residents Susan and John Munro. On this occasion, Trump's security team were given a full adult warning for breach of the peace. The tides were turning. Because whilst officialdom largely ignored complaints from Michael Forbes, it was he – not the Donald – who became a people's hero. Quite literally.

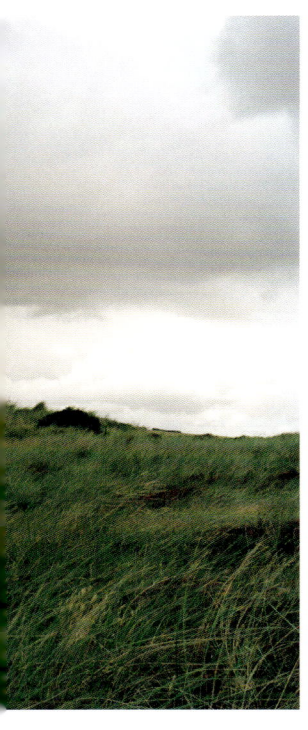
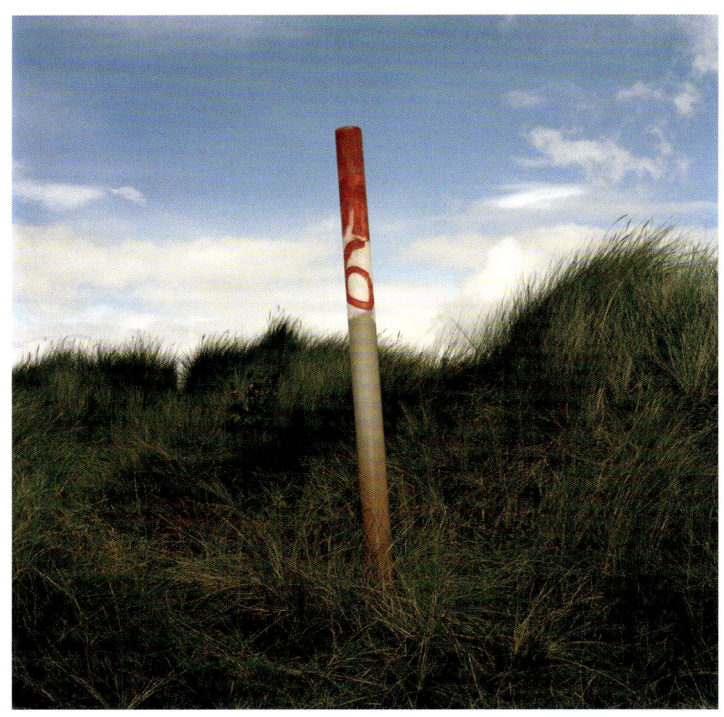
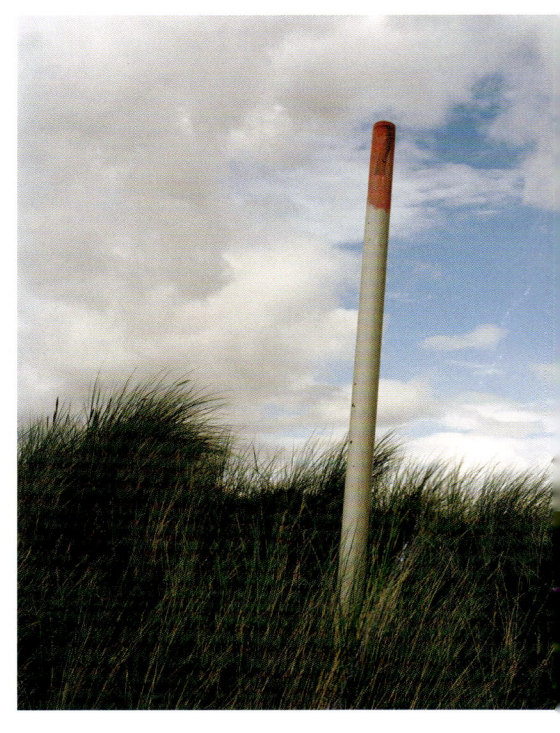
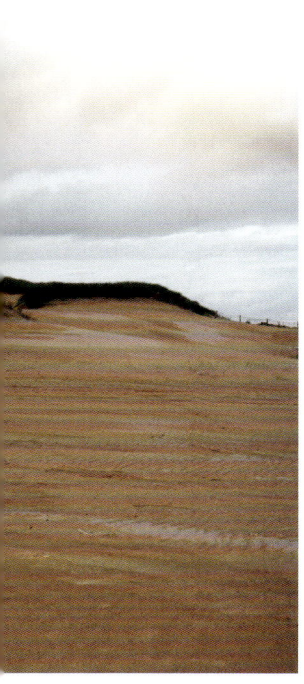
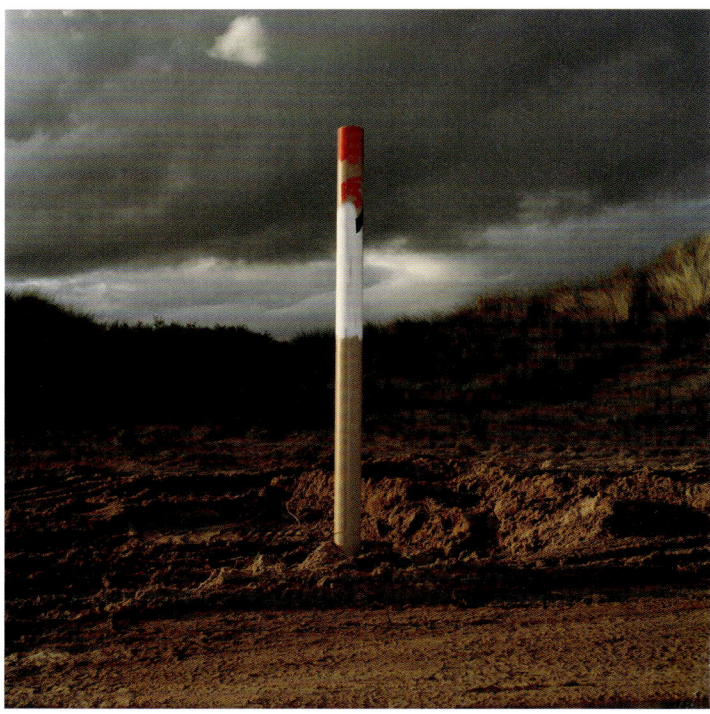
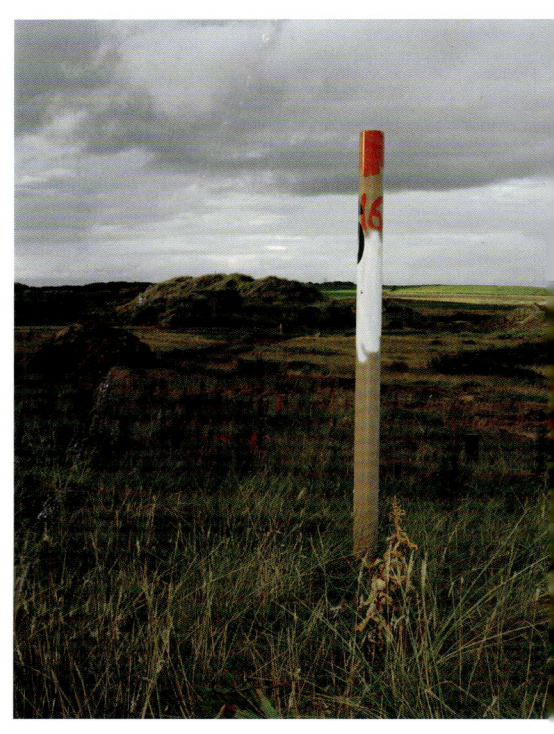

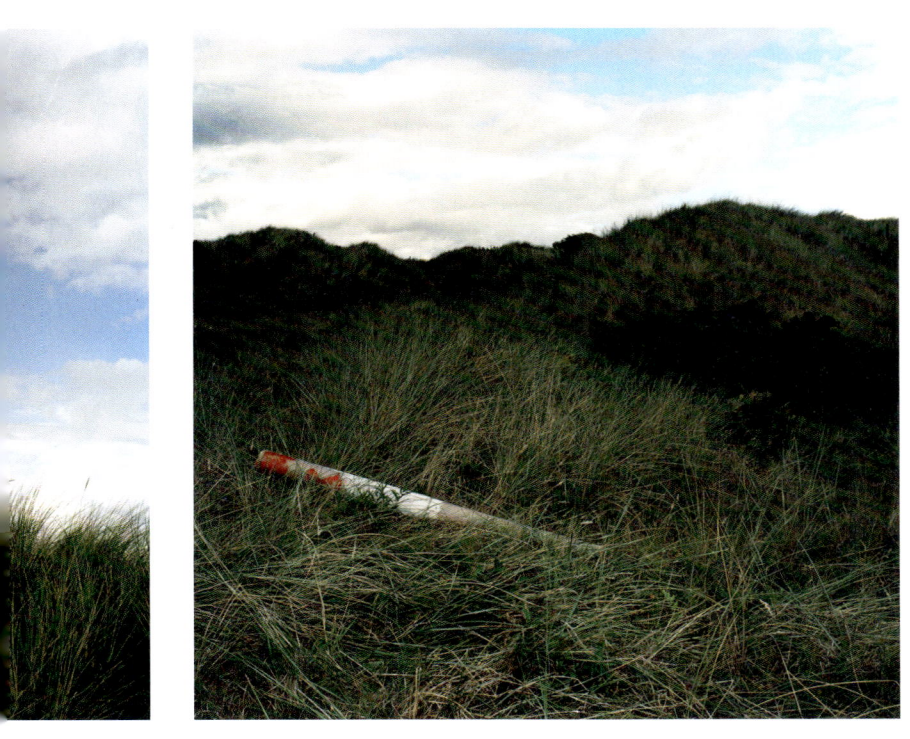
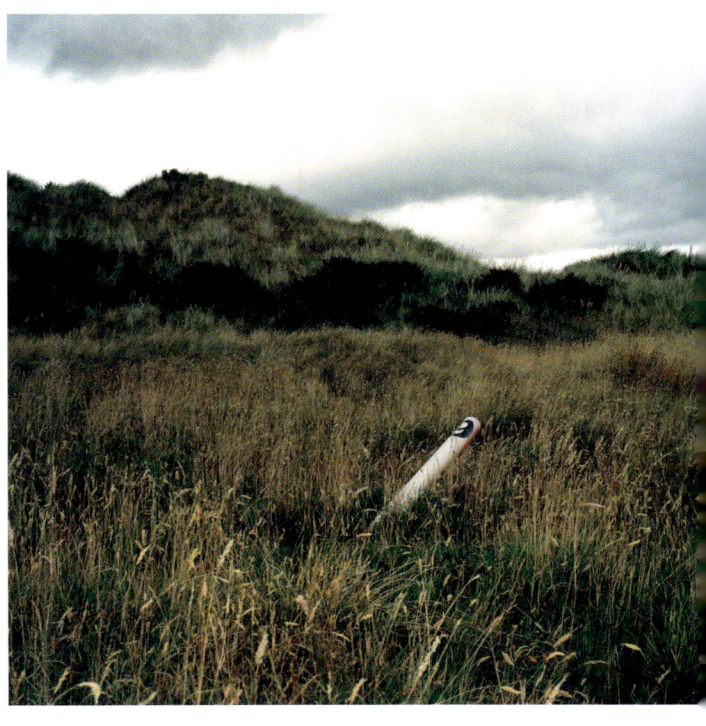
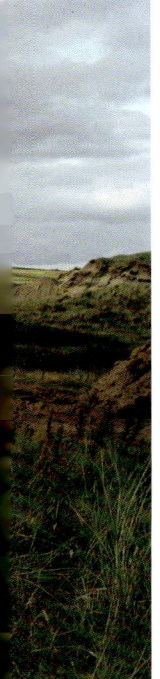
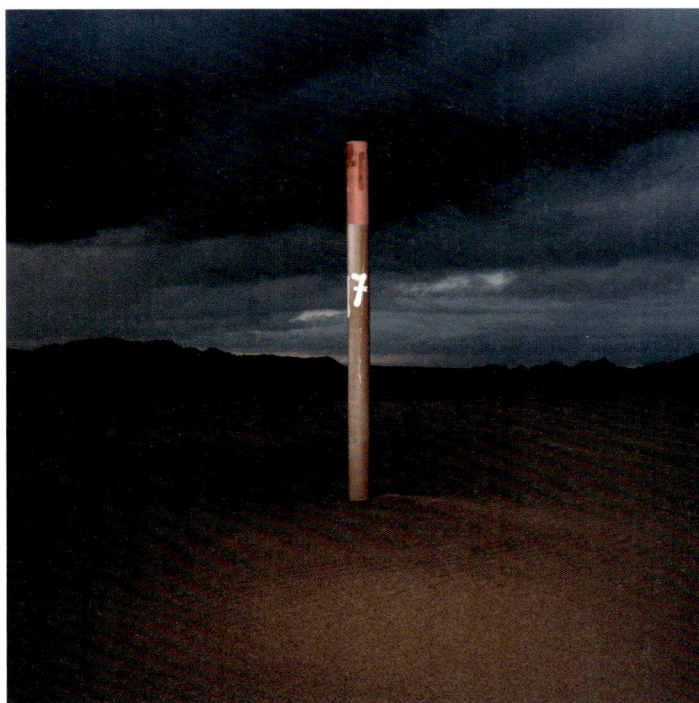
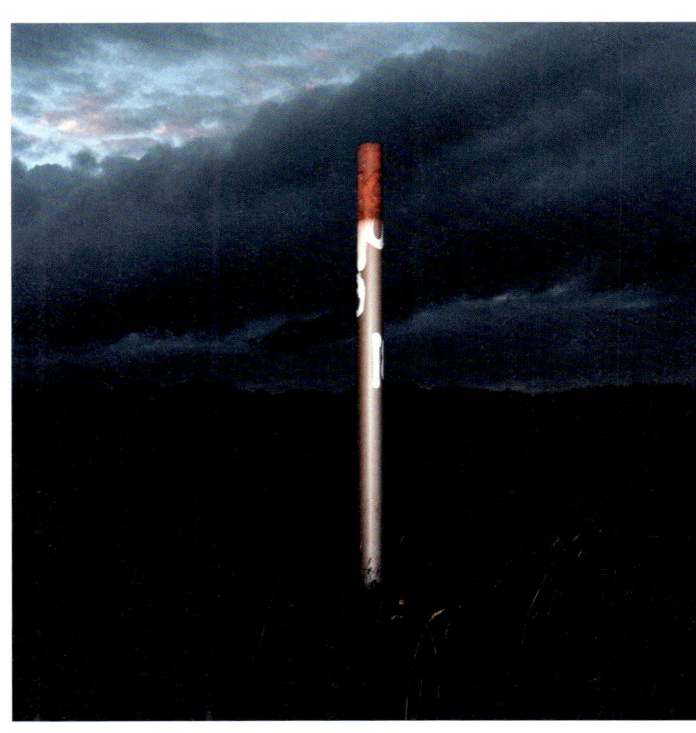

COMMENTARY

by Lesley Riddoch

Ah, Donald.

Ten years after your Trump International Golf Links opened for business on the Menie Estate in Aberdeenshire, you haven't crushed or removed the people who still dare to live on 'your' land. Perhaps that's because you haven't been the first to try.

In the long, long list of foreign owners who've spent wadges of cash to buy fiefdoms and the illusion of total feudal control, you are a relative newcomer. Folk across Scotland have long, bitter experience of lofty, self-interested operators like you – people whose changing fortunes and passing whims have helped shape or destroy thousands of lives.

As you were losing your first billion in 1994, the company charged with selling the North Lochinver Estate across in Sutherland was having a bad year too. Keen to wring the maximum profit from epic mountains and classic views, with stags and salmon in abundance, it planned to sell the 21,000-acre tranche of wild moor and lochans in seven lots – splitting one single, interconnected crofting community across seven new (and doubtless absentee) landowners. Assynt folk were angry and upset. Though quiet people accustomed to playing second fiddle, they were nonetheless insulted to the core by this offhand treatment of their families, livelihoods, and traditions.

The snub galvanised crofters, who were already bound together in the local branch of the Crofters' Union. They organised,

got publicity, deterred other bidders, and in 1993 the Assynt Crofters became the first in history to buy back their land from a laird on the open market. Four years later, across the choppy Minch, the people of Eigg did the same. The floodgates opened and have yet to close – today, half a million acres are in community control. On the Outer Hebrides, 70% of islanders now live on community-owned land. That's quite a turnaround, as two centuries earlier, locals had actually been banned from leaving the islands, lest the laird have no one to gather the kelp harvest. But when that market collapsed, the people were surplus to requirements, evicted and shipped out like human flotsam and jetsam. That's why the near-complete reversal of fortunes on the community-owned Western Isles tastes so sweet today. That same community control could have happened in Aberdeenshire and on Donald Trump's Menie Estate.

In the Victorian era, Aberdeenshire folk were well organised. 6,000 tenants and crofters met in the Granite City in 1881 to set up the Scottish Farmers Alliance (later the Scottish Land Reform Alliance), pushing for security of tenure and an end to feudal control. Two years later the Highland Land Law Reform Association was set up in Fraserburgh. Before the Crofters Act became law in 1886, Aberdeenshire crofters burned an effigy of one particularly despised laird, Alexander Burnett of Kemnay – twenty short miles from Trump's modern empire at Balmedie.

I was in the audience in 2012 when Michael beat Andy Murray, in a public vote, to win the Top Scot award at the Glenfiddich Spirit of Scotland Awards in Edinburgh. A shocked Trump immediately banned the brand from all of his properties and called for a worldwide boycott, prompting an avalanche of celebrities to raise defiant glasses of Glenfiddich on social media. That humiliation doubtless explained Trump's petty decision to put tariffs on Scottish whisky when he became president – a terrible episode in world history that is hopefully behind us.

In 2013, during Scotland's Climate Week, Alicia's photographs of Menie were exhibited in the Scottish Parliament, and First Minister Alex Salmond met with Michael Forbes the day after seeing the exhibition and meeting Alicia. This was a significant event because it was Salmond who had overturned the local council's rejection of Trump's plans, letting Trump International go ahead. Who knows what full and frank discussions might have occurred?

Afterwards, another Menie resident, David Milne, launched a petition calling for a public inquiry into the handling of Trump's development. The petition was lodged at the Scottish Parliament in March with 12,850 signatures. By the time the petition was heard, the number had grown to almost 20,000. The public inquiry was not granted, but the support for it was evident.

Trump is currently under investigation in the US for allegedly using fraudulent valuations of his Aberdeenshire golf resort to obtain loans, insurance coverage, and tax deductions. Federal investigators are on his trail and hopes are high he will be convicted and has thus blown any chance of regaining the Republican presidential nomination in 2024.

 Meanwhile, eleven of the world's most powerful wind turbines are steadily turning off the coast at Balmedie, despite Trump's five-year campaign to stop them 'spoiling his view'. And last year the 'Greatest Golf Course in the World' lost money again – for the eighth year in a row. Maybe its fortunes will recover. But the land will not be so lucky.

The dunes at Balmedie have lost their status as a protected Site of Special Scientific Interest. According to NatureScot, "There is now no longer a reason to protect the dunes at Menie as they do not include enough of the special natural features for which they were designated."

It took a decade for expert warnings to come true. It took ten minutes for savvy locals to size and sort Donald Trump. Maybe one day the great and good of Scotland will get over their admiration of arrogant outsiders and trust the local people who get it right, instantly, time after time.

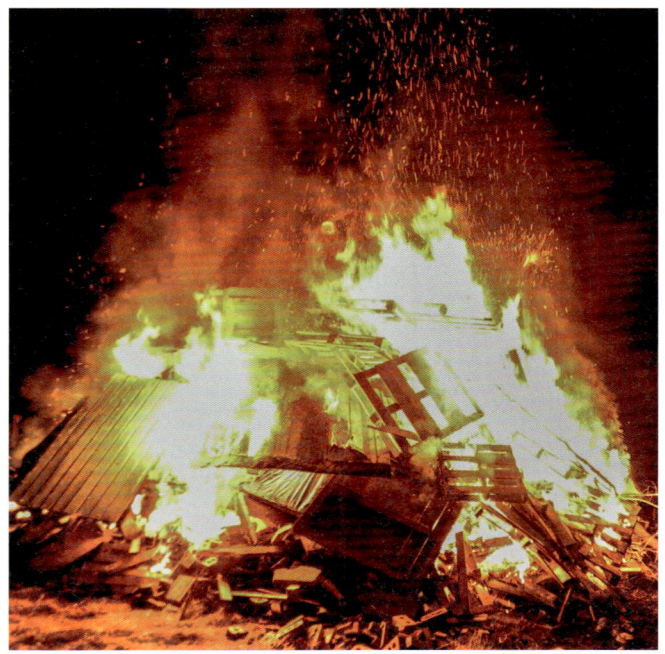

Menie bonfire, November 2012.

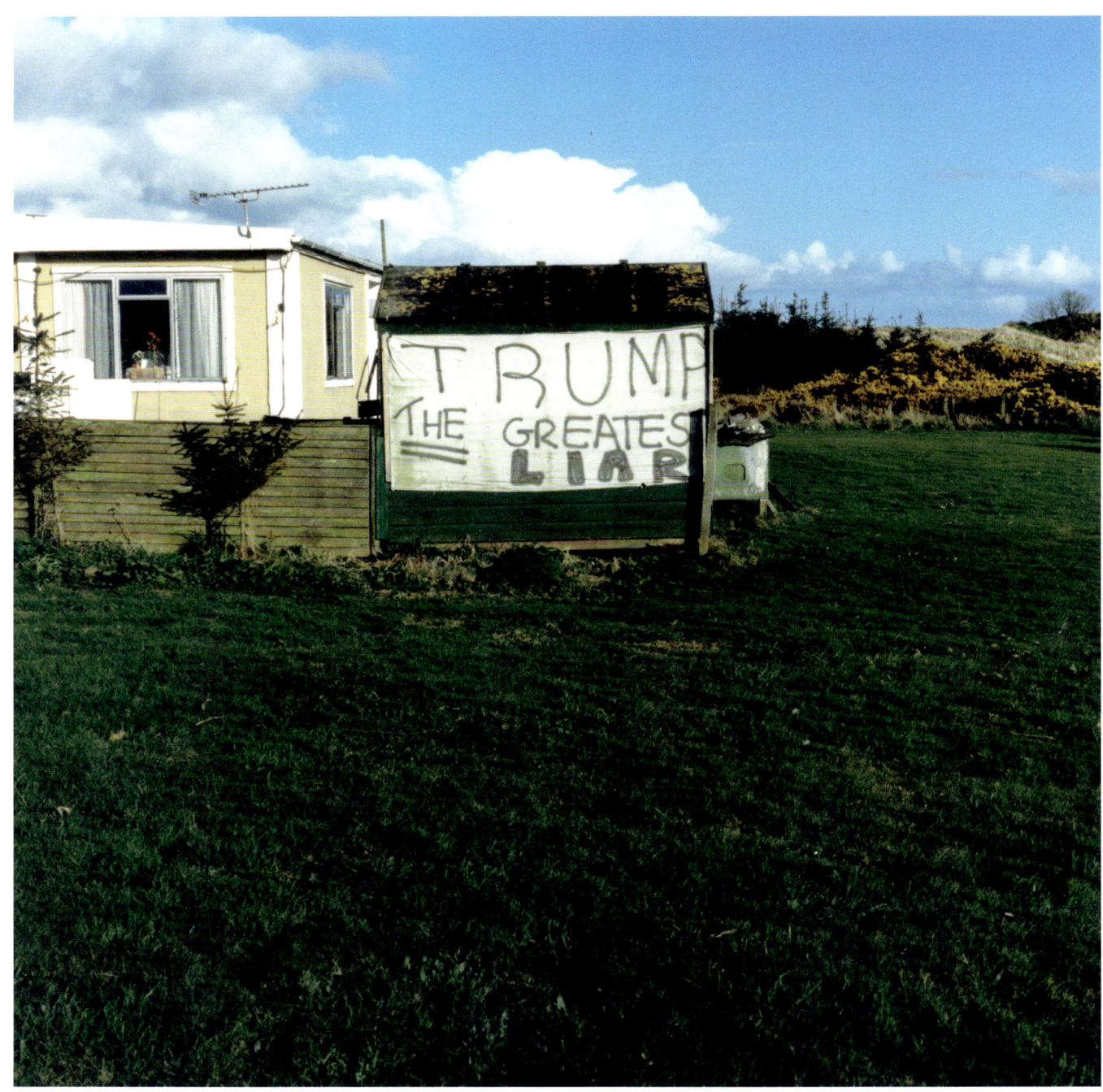

Trump the Greatest Liar: Chicken Shed at Paradise, the home of Molly Forbes, 2010.

SCOTTISH PHOTOGRAPHY WAS BORN OUT OF DISRUPTION

by Louise Pearson

Trump knew what he wanted and he expected to get it. To him, the people living in Menie were an inconvenience. A voiceless, faceless group of people who were in the way.

The residents of Menie aren't celebrities, but they deserve to be known. What started as a personal battle to protect their homes and community came to symbolise a much bigger struggle against a bully who operated in a global playground. Their fight made headlines and they became harder to ignore.

Alicia Bruce's photographs give that fight longevity. Newspaper headlines pass, but their story is preserved. Mike, Sheila, and Molly Forbes have become part of our national narrative. Their portraits were acquired by the National Galleries of Scotland in 2011 and have been displayed at the Scottish National Portrait Gallery alongside – and with equal importance to – notable Scots including Robert Burns, Annie Lennox, and Mary, Queen of Scots. Future residents of Menie will know how they fought for their corner of the Scottish coast.

And this is a form of protest. A quiet, dignified act of rebellion. Because Trump is proud of his Scottish heritage, that his mother came from the Isle of Lewis. Instead of a glorious entrance into the nation's collective memory as president of the United States and successful business tycoon, his mark on Scotland is remembered by his poor treatment of its citizens and the destruction of its unique landscape. The motherland won't forget.

A fuller record of Alicia Bruce's journey with the Forbes family and their neighbours is held by the University of St Andrews. Mixed with portraits of a community fighting back are images which capture the destruction of a peaceful stretch of coast – the

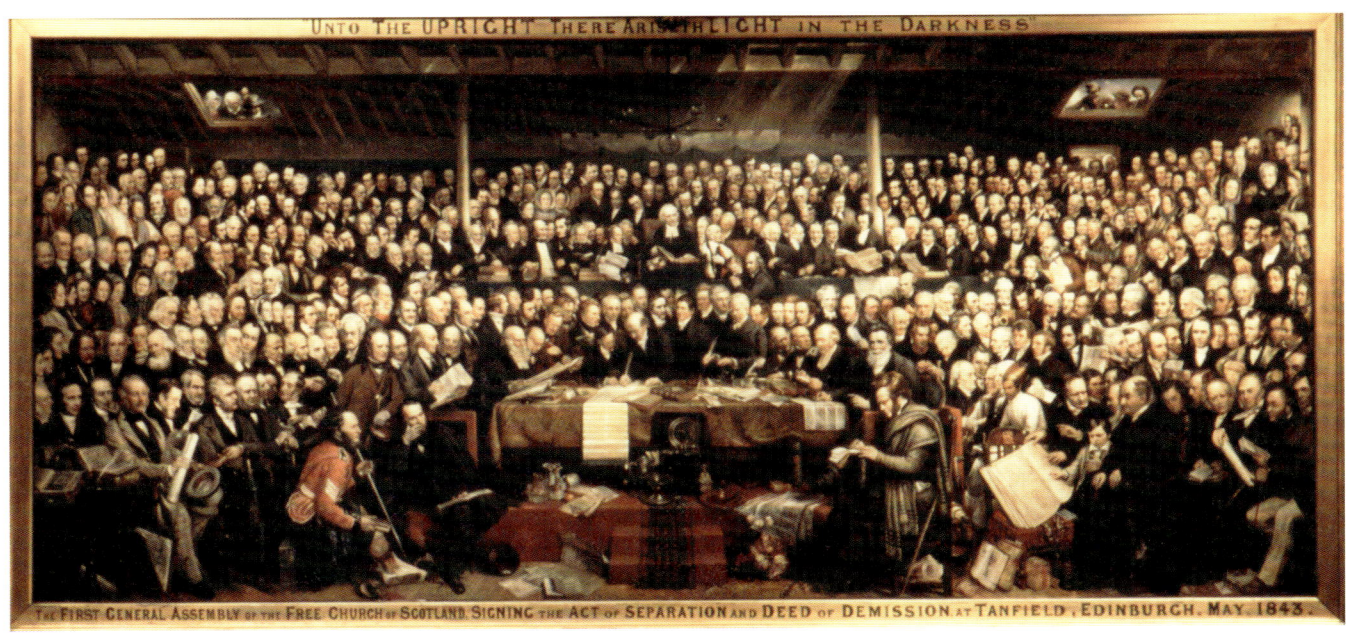

David Octavius Hill RSA, *The First General Assembly of the Free Church of Scotland, signing the Act of Separation and Deed of Demission – 18ᵗʰ May 1843*.

brutal arrival of a digger, the abrupt end to a new tarmac track. There is an irony in these photographs being preserved in the home of golf and the home of Scottish photography.

Public art collections are increasingly looking to reflect experiences beyond those of celebrities. It is no longer enough to focus on great art and famous faces. The world is in a period of turbulence, our lives shaped by inequality, economic uncertainty, climate anxiety, and political unrest. Galleries are a place to reflect, to process. The art we see should resonate with our experiences and inspire change. Alicia Bruce's photographs do that. They document a moment in time, a particular fight, but they speak to a common aspiration – having the guts to fight for what you believe in.

And now there is this book. More than ten years have passed since Alicia Bruce first met the residents of Menie, and in that time Trump has risen to president of the United States and crashed back down again. Millions of people have been affected by his whims. Many more communities have suffered. The

defiance of a small Scottish community has a greater resonance now than we could ever have imagined. A taste of what was to come – a warning sign to America. This book is a permanent record of Menie's part in raising the alarm.

Photographers have always been drawn to people making a stand. To stories of communities pulling together. Scottish photography was born out of disruption. The famous partnership of David Octavius Hill and Robert Adamson formed as a practical way to capture the likeness of the hundreds of ministers involved in the foundation of the Free Church of Scotland. These men had given up their churches, incomes, and homes in protest at state intervention in the Church. Hill's monumental *Disruption* painting presents the ministers as equals – reflective of the democratic nature of the newly formed Church and the new medium of photography.

Alicia Bruce twists the dialogue between historic paintings and photography back on itself. Her portrait of Mike and Sheila

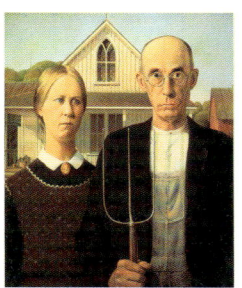

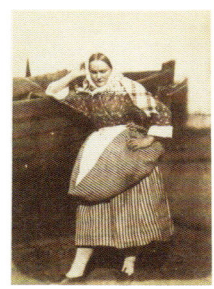

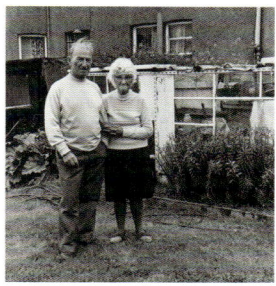

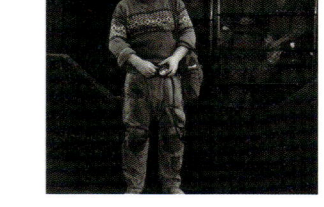

Grant Wood, *American Gothic*, 1930. Friends of American Art Collection, Art Institute of Chicago.

David Octavius Hill and Robert Adamson, *Jeanie Wilson [Newhaven 15]*, 1843–1857. National Galleries of Scotland.

Milton Rogovin, *Family of Miners (1981–1990) Scotland*. National Galleries of Scotland.

Forbes is a homage to Grant Wood's iconic painting *American Gothic*, which resides in the collection of the Art Institute of Chicago. Grit and determination radiate from the Forbeses as they stand in front of the house Trump has threatened to destroy. The choice of painting taps into this battle of wills in a myriad of ways. It has been parodied many times – much like Trump. It evokes ordinary people defending their land and their way of life. It brings American culture to Scotland, and it elevates Mike and Sheila Forbes to figures worthy of inclusion in the history of art.

This is a common theme in photography – the placing of ordinary people at the forefront of art. It is telling that, having completed their initial task, Hill and Adamson turned their attention to the fishing community of Newhaven. This would become their most admired body of work, celebrated as the start of documentary photography. They had recognised something in photography that sets it apart from other art forms – its ability to connect with communities and share their stories.

This is particularly true of communities struggling. Many photographers seem to have an innate sense of justice. A desire to use their talent to elevate others and to hold people – or organisations – to account. American photographer Milton Rogovin did this throughout his career, giving working people a platform to share the reality of their lives. His series *Family of Miners*, made over the course of two decades, shows that people around the world – from China to Scotland, Zimbabwe to Spain – were facing the same challenges. The series puts faces to newspaper stories of unemployment, ill health, and changing government policies. Alicia Bruce is following in this tradition, ensuring the preservation of our shared history.

Photographers can only effectively communicate on behalf of a community if there is trust on both sides, and this is evident in Alicia Bruce's portraits of the residents of Menie. They trust her to tell their story and she has a genuine concern for their well-being. This relationship has developed over many years. She has shared in their initial disbelief, their early rallying of support, the days that felt hopeless, and the years when it felt like the world was starting to understand why they were standing up to Trump. She has mourned with them as a friend. The durability of this relationship is what makes this series of photographs a success.

Alicia Bruce was the right person to tell this story. She got it. She knew the landscape from childhood and felt a connection to the people through a shared working-class background. She felt the anger they felt and she had the drive to join their protest.

Arts organisations around the world are – belatedly – making more room for photographers like Alicia Bruce. There is now an acknowledgment that there shouldn't be a mould for the type of artists who are celebrated. We need to see more working-class women working in photography, just as we need to see more photographers from other underrepresented groups. Diversity is essential if we are to amplify the voices that need to be heard.

You can tear these dunes asunder,
pound this wonder into dust,
with your cruel hands and crooked hearts,
laden with lust and expensive lies,
but the haar* will stumble in to cover your eyes,

the haar will stumble in.

—from 'Cover Your Eyes'
by Karine Polwart & Steven Polwart

*Haar (Scots): sea mist, a familiar weather feature of Scotland's North Sea coast.

AFTERWORD

by Karine Polwart

In the early summer of 2011, documentary filmmaker Anthony Baxter asked me to sing at the debut Scottish screening of *You've Been Trumped*, a film documenting the contested development of the Trump International Golf Links on the Menie Estate. The Trump course had by then become a David and Goliath media saga in Scotland, sparking protest around environmental protection, democratic decision-making, and the power of big money.

Sitting on a unique dynamic coastal dune system, previously designated a Site of Special Scientific Interest, the essence of Balmedie was, and still is, instability and flux, and an openness to the harsh maritime conditions of Aberdeenshire's North Sea coast.

Balmedie is also a place where people live. The individual stories of its residents, the small details of their family lives, and their emotional connection to the land, is what moved me most about Anthony's documentary. My own children were five and two at the time, so watching Susan Munro with an old photograph in hand, recalling the joy of paddling on Balmedie beach with her children and her mother, got to me. "You realise what you've got and what's going to be taken away," she says in the film.

Mickey Foote's reminiscences of his own childhood touched me, too. "I used to come up here with my grandmother and my aunt and my cousins, on the bus from Aberdeen, with our bandy catchers[1], and play commandos on those dunes," he tells Anthony. "It was a fantastic open space within reach of ordinary people," he says before adding, "The only wild stretch has been swallowed up in this development."

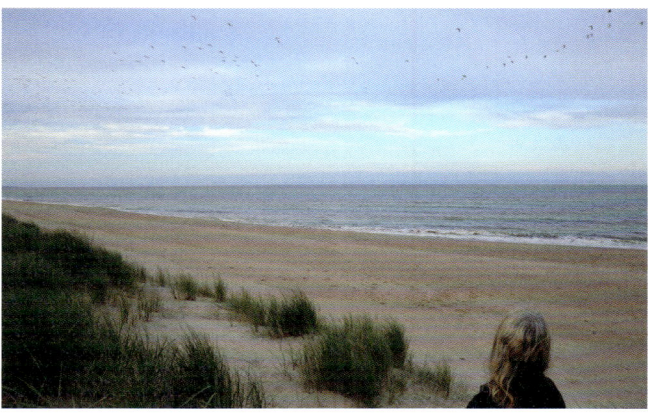

Susan Munro on Menie beach, 2010.

With advance access to Anthony's rough cut of *You've Been Trumped*, and the voices of Susan and Mickey and their neighbours in my ears, I sat with my brother Steven and wrote 'Cover Your Eyes' for the film's Scottish premiere. In it, I imagine us as children in that landscape:

---

1 *Bandy catchers* (Scots): a small handheld fishing net; a 'bandy' is a stickleback.

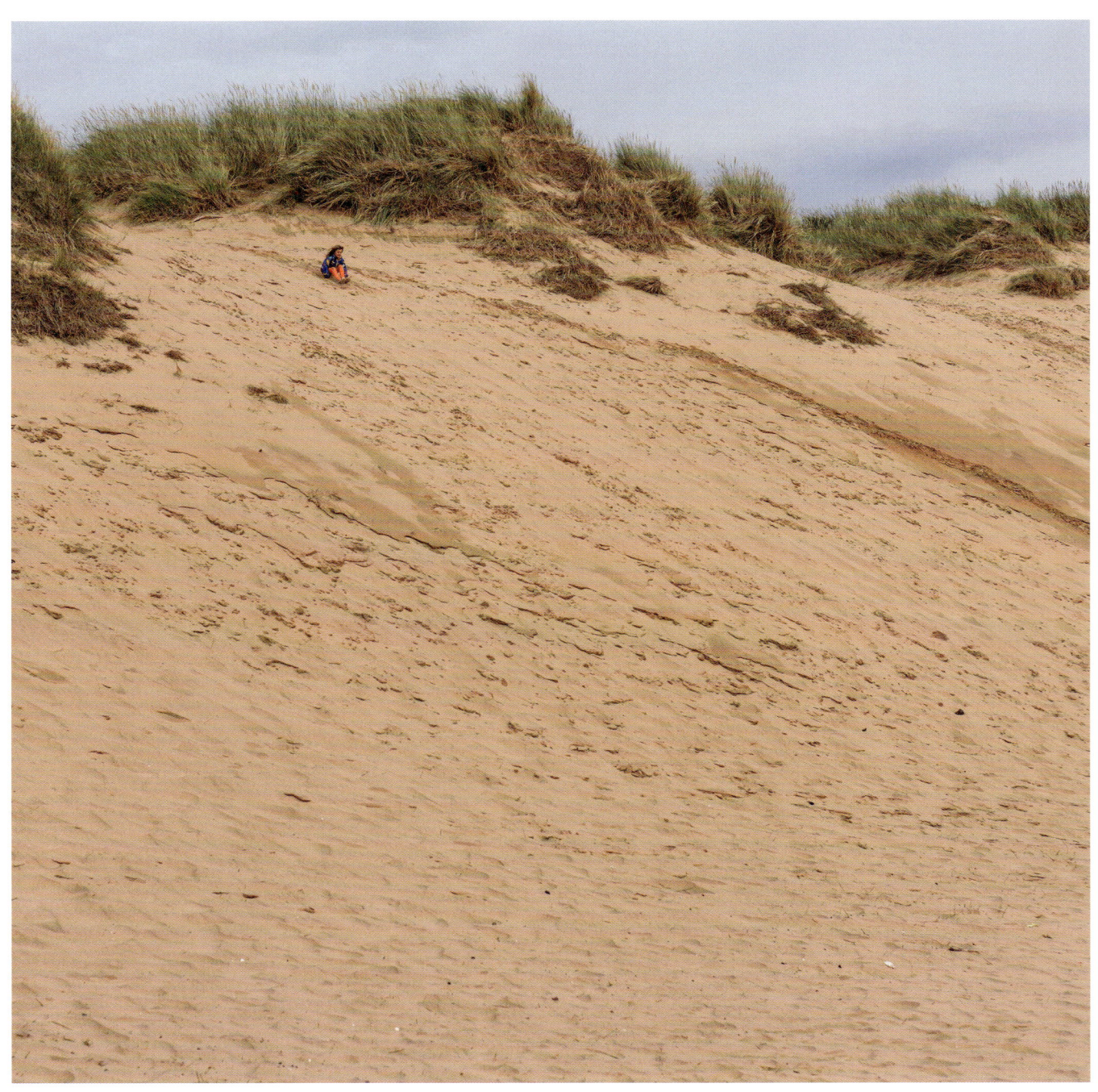

Alicia's young daughter playing in the sand dunes, Balmedie, July 2022.

I was Farrah Fawcett,
you were Steve McQueen
And we rode your silver Grifter[2]
half the way from Aberdeen
And the waves fall

I kept lookout in the marram grass
U-boats on the skyline,
commandos at the pass
And the waves fall

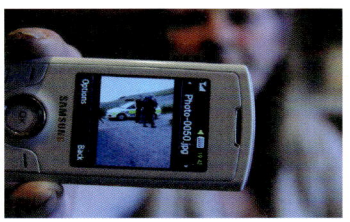

Susan Munro with her camera-phone image of 30 July 2010. Journalists Anthony Baxter and Richard Phinney were arrested at her home whilst making the documentary *You've Been Trumped*. Police officers PC Wilkinson and PC McKay told them to turn their camera off. They were detained under Section 14 of the Criminal Procedure (Scotland) Act 1995.

You've Been Trumped introduced me to some of the images on the pages of this book, via scenes from the opening of Alicia's first Menie exhibition at Peacock Visual Arts in Aberdeen in January 2011. It's clear from the footage, and from the wider film itself, how much it matters to Balmedie residents to be seen and dignified by artists like Alicia and Anthony.

Our emotional connections to place have huge significance in our embodied lives but almost no value at all in our civic and political decision-making. This is true most especially of the places which children and families know and love, where we walk our dogs, play hide and seek, or lie looking at the stars. It's precisely this everyday, human-scale meaning, the way in which people are *of* place, which Alicia's portraits of Menie residents evoke so powerfully.

Anthony's documentary film and Alicia's photography led the way as artistic responses to the Trump International Golf Links

2 A Grifter was a prized 1980s kids' bike.

project and helped to bring both its environmental and human consequences to wider public and political attention. I first met Alicia on 24 April 2012 at a special showing of *You've Been Trumped* at the Scottish Parliament in Edinburgh. The screening was timed to coincide with Trump's testimony to a Scottish parliamentary commit-

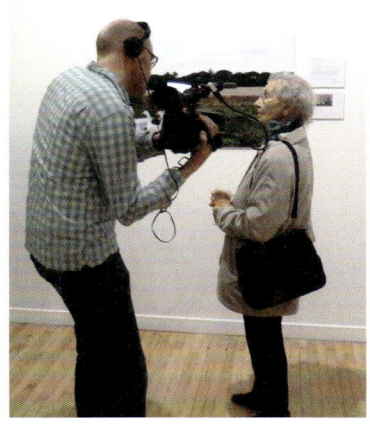

Anthony Baxter filming Molly Forbes with Alicia's photograph of her at Peacock Visual Arts, Aberdeen, 14 August 2021.

tee on wind farms. Trump was, of course, virulently opposed to a proposed North Sea turbine site three miles offshore from his executive clubhouse at Menie. When asked to present evidence that the wind farm development would decimate local tourism income, he saw no irony at all in citing its adverse impact on the landscape, and declaring, memorably, "I am the evidence."

Trump was by then a figure of considerable national derision in Scotland. But within a couple of years, no one was laughing.

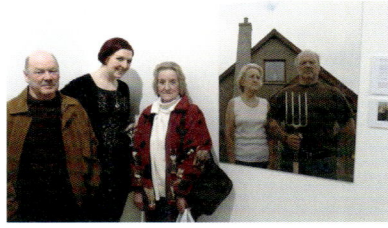

Alicia Bruce with Mike and Sheila Forbes, Peacock Visual Arts, 14 January 2011.

In the week following the US presidential election of 2016, I was approached by Celtic Connections Festival in Glasgow, the largest winter arts festival in Europe, to perform with the BBC Scottish Symphony Orchestra at the opening event of their upcoming 2017 programme. The proposed date was 20 January, the eve of Donald Trump's presidential inauguration.

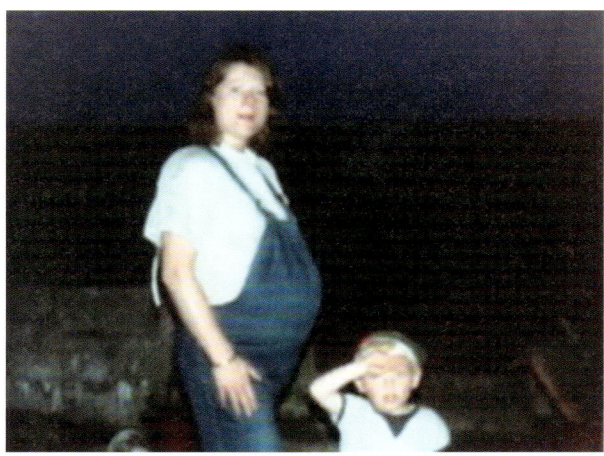

Susan pregnant with Finlay, with her older son Murdo, Leyton Cottage, early 1980s. Screenshot from *You've Been Trumped*, Dir Anthony Baxter, 2011.

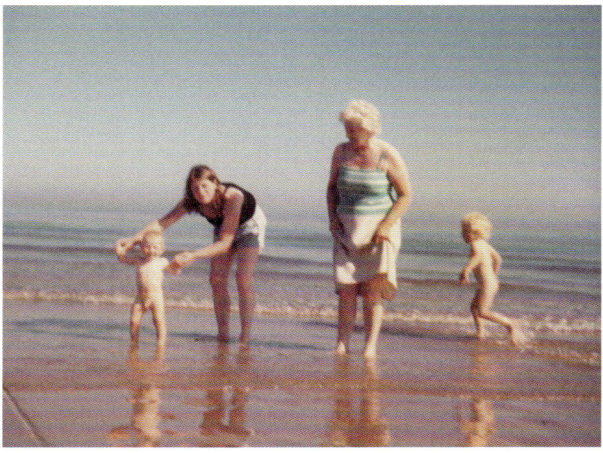

Susan Munro with her sons Murdo and Finlay and her mother paddling on Menie Beach, early 1980s. Photograph courtesy of John Munro.

I replied to the festival with one condition: I'd be honoured to perform, but I'd like the opening slot of the programme, please. I knew I had something to say.

The result is a part-spoken, part-sung piece called 'I Burn but I Am Not Consumed', which lends its name also to this collection of Alicia's work. Its voice is that of the greater-than-human world, the ancient Hebridean rock of Trump's maternal ancestors, the land which came before us, and which will outlast us all, whatever the human power, vanity, and destructiveness of now.

At this time of profound climate crisis and social injustice, I wonder what values might underpin our lives, and speak to what really matters for the global majority of us, if we lived in embodied awareness of the short span of humanity's existence.

Meanwhile, I'll let the rock of Lewis speak for itself.

I BURN BUT I AM NOT CONSUMED

On 11 May 1930, Mary Anne MacLeod, from Tong on the Isle of Lewis, boarded the RMS Transylvania from Glasgow to New York City, in search of a better life. There, she fell in love with Frederick, whose father had come to America from Germany two generations before. The couple raised five children.

Mary Anne's middle son would return years later to Scotland, home of his MacLeod ancestors, whose clan motto is 'I Burn but I Am Not Consumed'. And here, in the name of progress and profit, and executive golf, he would pit himself against time and tide. In his wake, the shifting sands at Balmedie in Aberdeenshire would never be the same.

That son of Mary Anne MacLeod is powerful.

But so, too, is the North Wind.

The marbled, metamorphic rock of Lewis is two-thirds the age of Earth, amongst the very oldest found on our planet. It knows about power. And it's seen a lot. And, so, I wondered: What might that rock of Lewis have to say about the inauguration of the 45th president of the United States of America, Mary Anne MacLeod's middle son, Donald John?

This is what the rock told me:

Oh son of Lewis, lonely boy,
hewn from granite, salt and sky
upon a foreign shore:
the ocean is a mirror gleam
in which you see yourself,
and nothing more.

Three billion years of gravity,
of strata forged in fire and earth,
the stone crib of your mother's birth,
in which your forebears lie.
I am alive. I am a tomb.
I burn, but I am not consumed.
I burn, but I am not consumed.

Fish may swim at your command
across the Atlantic to the land
of dreams and self-belief and boundless chance.
An exile tale.
An immigrant dance.
You're captain of a frigate now,
So set your compass, raise the mast,
Blow up the sails, erase the past,
and future, if you must.
Together we can stand
and watch the peat-land turn to dust.

This is your apprenticeship:
The Gulf Stream doesn't know your name,
nor does the splendid, blazing sun
that alters how the currents run.
The North Wind never heard you roar:
You're fired! You're fired!
My back might burn, and the blaze run wild,
but I am not consumed, my child.

The Minch whips up a spindrift storm.
The machair[3] *shifts. The machair moans.*
At Uig Bay and Luskentyre,
the gale blows fast, the tide flows higher.
The shore erodes and disappears.
And, meantime, you are stoking fears
and stacking hope into a pyre.
You strike a match.

Oh ma bairn[4]*, mo leanaibh*[5]
Oh ma bairn, mo leanaibh

Your mother was a wee girl once,
who played upon my rocky shore.
And you, you are a broken boy,
and you want more and more and more.
You build a tower.
You build a wall.
You live in fear that they might fall.
You who see nothing but your face
in the sheen of the Hudson River.

---

3 *Machair* (Scottish Gaelic): a fertile, low-lying, coastal grassy plain of NW Ireland and Scotland, esp. the Western Isles.
4 *Ma bairn* (Scots): child.
5 *Mo leanaibh* (Scottish Gaelic): my child.

Oh ma bairn, mo leanaibh
Oh ma bairn, mo leanaibh

A balancing is yet to come,
although by then you may be gone
and leave a desert to your sons and daughters.
Still, these waters, they will rise,
the North Sea haar will cover your eyes,
despite your disregard for truth
and your appetite for lies.

Three billion years of gravity,
of strata forged in fire and earth,
the stone crib of your mother's birth,
in which your forebears lie.
I am alive. I am a tomb.
I burn, but I am not consumed.
I burn, but I am not consumed. [6]

6 A recording of 'I Burn but I Am Not Consumed' is available on *Laws of Motion* by Karine Polwart with Steven Polwart and Inge Thomson (Hudson Records, 2018) and via a live performance on NPR's Tiny Desk Concerts. 'Cover Your Eyes' is the opening track of Karine Polwart's album *Traces* (Hegri Music, 2012).

I BURN BUT
I AM NOT CONSUMED

Timeline

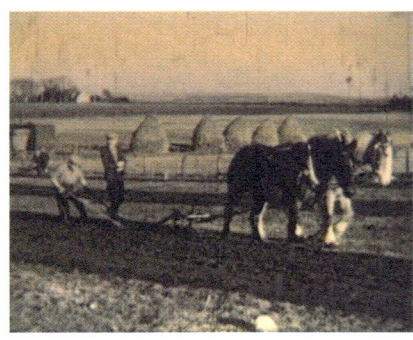 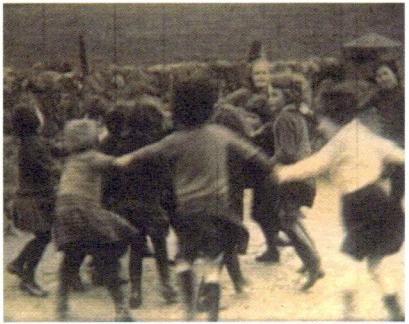

Molly Forbes's father ploughing (left) and Menie School.
(*Belhelvie Jubilee Gazette*, 1935, Scotland's Moving Image Archive.)

2006

12 January

First suggestions that Trump aides are in talks with Aberdeenshire Council.

31 March

Donald Trump announces plans for a £1bn golf complex, revealing that he has bought Menie Estate, of which he says he has "never seen such a non-spoiled and dramatic seaside landscape and the location makes it perfect for our development."

3 April

First Minister Jack McConnell meets Trump at a Tartan Week event in New York. McConnell's opponents from the Scottish Green Party accuse him of breaching the ministerial code. The claims are denied.

28–30 April

Donald Trump visits Scotland to tour the site.

26 November

Incomplete planning application lodged with Aberdeenshire Council, but vital documents will not be sent until March 2007. This means planners cannot write a report assessing the merits of the project until after then.

27 November

Trump unveils £1bn golfing plans to build the "greatest golf course in the world" in Menie to the press.

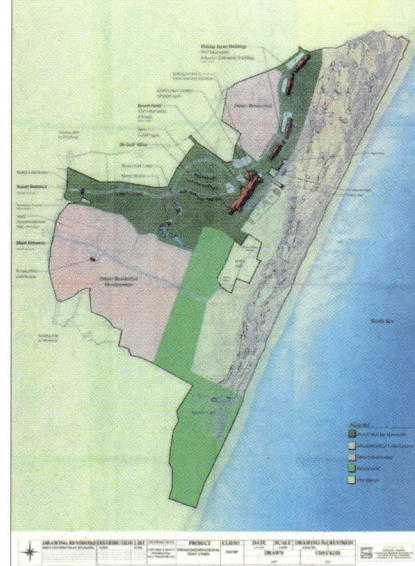

Trump development designs.

2005

June

Tom Griffin, owner of the Menie Estate, meets golf course developer Neil Hobday.

September

Scottish Development International staff flies with Hobday to New York to deliver a presentation at Trump Tower. Hobday bids for Tom Griffin's land without naming his backer, so it won't drive up the price.

October

First Minister Jack McConnell meets Donald Trump at Trump Tower HQ in New York.

2007

30 March

Planning application is completed by lodging of missing documents. The full planning application is submitted. Concerns are raised about environmental impact.

11 September

Aberdeenshire planning officials recommend that councillors approve the golf resort.

September

Sustainable Aberdeen, the first group to oppose Trump, is formed.

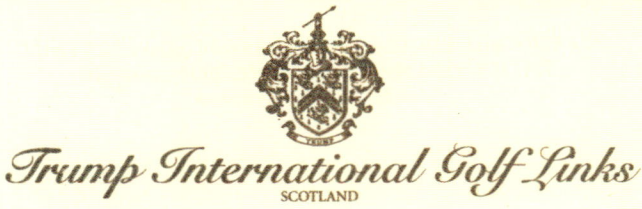

Trump International Golf Links
SCOTLAND

Your personal invitation to 'Share our Vision'

As one of our neighbours, you are cordially invited to come along to Forsyth Hall, Belhelvie Church, Balmedie, AB23 8YR to share in our vision for Trump International Golf Links, Scotland. We are currently in the planning phase of the development and we would be delighted to share the initial plans with you.

Please join us on Tuesday 28th November 2006.

You have the option to join us at one of two events:

Option 1
14.00 – Arrival Reception
14.30 – Video and Presentation from Ashley Cooper, The Trump Organization
15.15 – Q&A Session with Panel
15.30 – Finish

Option 2
18.30 – Arrival Reception
19.00 – Video and Presentation from Ashley Cooper, The Trump Organization
19.45 – Q&A Session with Panel
20.00 – Finish

INVITES ARE FOR ADDRESSEES ONLY AND WILL BE REQUIRED TO BE PRODUCED FOR ADMITTANCE TO FORSYTH HALL

Numbers are limited so please RSVP as soon as possible to let us know if you wish to attend and at which time.

Should you require transportation to and from the event, please do advise us in writing or by email

RSVP in writing to:

Trump International Golf Links
Menie Park Lodge
Menie Estate
Balmedie
Aberdeen AB23 8YE

Or by Email – info@trumpgolfscotland.com

We very much look forward to seeing you at Forsyth Hall on 28th November 2006.

With kindest regards,

Lora McCluskey

Trump International Golf Links, Scotland

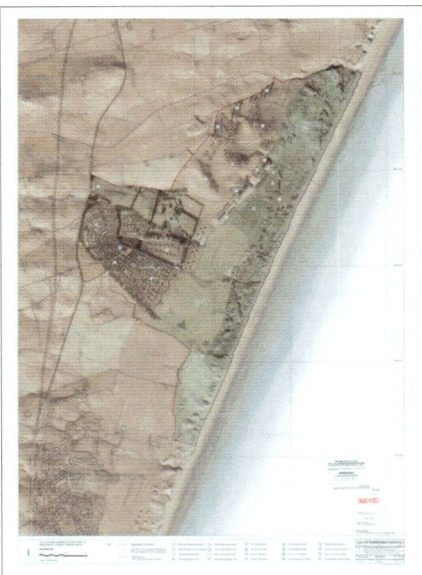

Trump development designs.

18 September

Formartine Area Committee of Aberdeenshire Council first considers the application.

27 September

The application goes before Formartine Area Committee at Balmedie Primary School.

20 November

Formartine meets and approves outline consent for the development.

29 November

Aberdeenshire Council's Infrastructure Services Committee votes to refuse the application. Councillor Martin Ford makes the casting vote to refuse consent.

30 November

The *Press and Journal* front page features Martin Ford and George Sorial. Sorial, Trump's legal representative, tells reporters: "I think it sends out a devastating message that, if you want to do big business, don't do it in the north-east of Scotland."

30 November

Evening Express front page 'You Traitors' headline seeks to reflect the sentiment that 97% of its readers surveyed backed the golf resort. The newspaper includes a cut-out poster stating 'Stuff the council neeps. We support Trump'. The editorial includes phrases such as 'betrayed by stupidity of seven', describing the councillors as 'small-minded numpties', 'misfits', 'buffoons in woolly jumpers', 'traitors to the north-east', and 'no-hopers'.

3 December

Trump announces he will not appeal the refused application.

4 December

Scottish Government calls in the application.

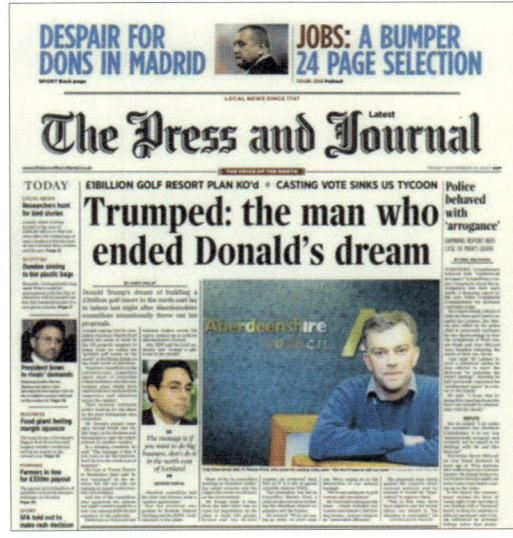

Front page of the *Press and Journal*, 30 November 2007.

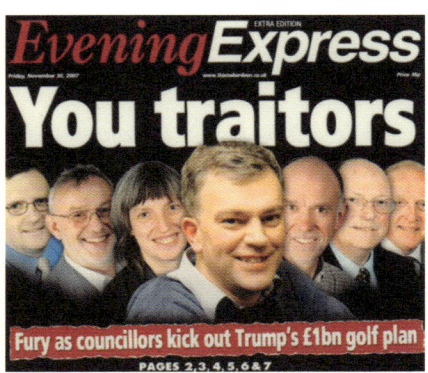

Front page of *Evening Express*,
30 November 2007.

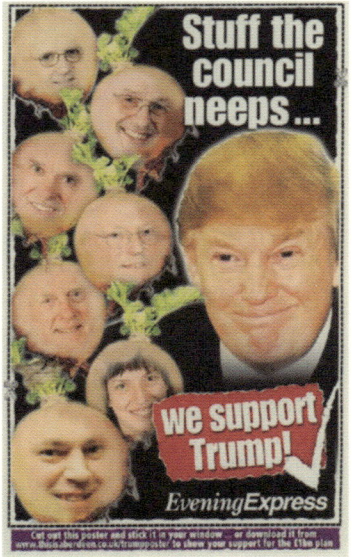

Evening Express cut-out poster 'Stuff the
Council Neeps', 30 November 2007.

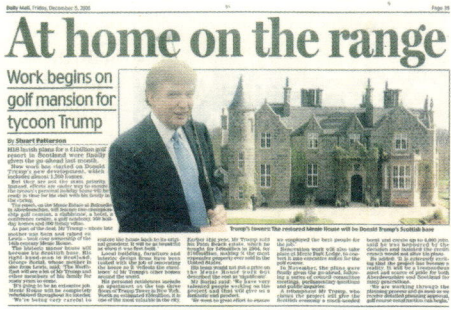

Daily Mail, Friday, 5 December 2008.

2008

9 December

First Minister Alex Salmond meets Trump representatives the day before ministers give their final say. He insists that because the plans fell into his Gordon constituency, he is duty-bound to meet people on all sides.

12 December

Councillor Martin Ford is sacked in a vote of no confidence from his role as chairman of the Infrastructure Services Committee.

12 December

Aberdeenshire Councillors give their overwhelming support for the development.

19 December

The Scottish Parliament's local government committee calls in plans and takes to a public inquiry. Questions are asked about First Minister Alex Salmond's meetings with Trump.

10 June

Public inquiry in Aberdeen. Trump gives evidence.

10 June

Donald Trump states at the public inquiry (10/06–04/07) that he has all the land he needs for his development, also describing the site as 'kind of disgusting'.

3 November

Consent is issued by Scottish Government to build a luxury golf resort.

2009

17 February

Draft of compulsory purchase orders (CPOs) by Ann Faulds, Head of Planning and Transportation, Dundas & Wilson law firm.

4 March

Trump International Golf Links Scotland (TIGLS) requests the Aberdeenshire Council use compulsory purchase powers for Menie residents' properties.

28 March

Aberdeenshire Councillor Debra Storr complains of 'thuggish' behaviour after she takes photographs of locked gates on the Menie Estate. Her car is blocked in by Trump security staff who are then ordered by police to let her go.

7 April

Director of Planning and Environmental Services responds in writing to Ann Faulds of Dundas & Wilson's correspondence concerning CPOs.

7 May

Letter from Trump to Milnes alerting them of planning permission.

8 September

Planning permission is granted.

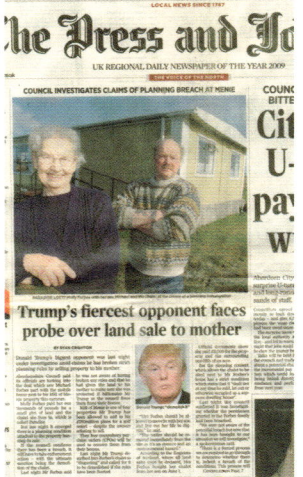

The *Press and Journal*, Wednesday, 3 November 2010.

18–19 September

A master-plan exhibition is hosted by Trump Scotland.

21 September

Letters are sent to David and Moira Milne offering £230,000 for their home, only a bit more than half of its market value.

30 September

Alex Salmond writes to David Milne, responding to Mr Milne's concerns about CPOs and explaining the official process.

1 October

Over 15,000 sign a petition organised by Tripping Up Trump against the use of a CPO at Menie.

1 October

Aberdeenshire Councillor Martin Ford moves a motion to oppose CPOs, but it is rejected.

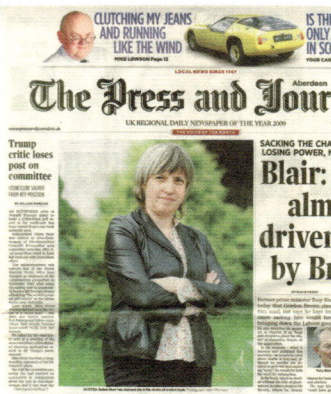

Debra Storr featured in the *Press and Journal*, Wednesday, 1 September 2010.

November

Molly Forbes launches a legal challenge in a bid to stop the building of the golf course on her land.

Work starts on stabilising the sand dunes.

2010

January

Molly Forbes loses the first round of her legal challenge to Trump.

January

Local primary-school children participate in an on-site workshop to plant marram grass to help stabilise the sand dunes.

2010 continued

February

A detailed master plan is submitted to the Aberdeenshire Council.

March

Design and Textile students from Gray's School of Art at Robert Gordon University are assigned an opportunity to design a tartan for Trump Scotland, with a fashion shoot at MacLeod House.

12 March

Menie resident David Milne is told to 'clear off' by Trump's project director Neil Hobday at a TIGLS planning exhibition at Udny Arms, Newburgh.

26 May

'The Bunker' goes live. Mike Forbes, via campaign group Tripping Up Trump, sells an acre of his land near Aberdeen to protesters who also disagree with Trump's plans – a sale which will force the property tycoon to face down more than sixty people. "Tripping Up Trump now own a piece of my land in an effort to help protect my family and the other families worried by the threat of compulsory purchase," Forbes says in a statement. "Trump lost the battle for public opinion long ago, and he's now lost any chance of bulldozing our homes."

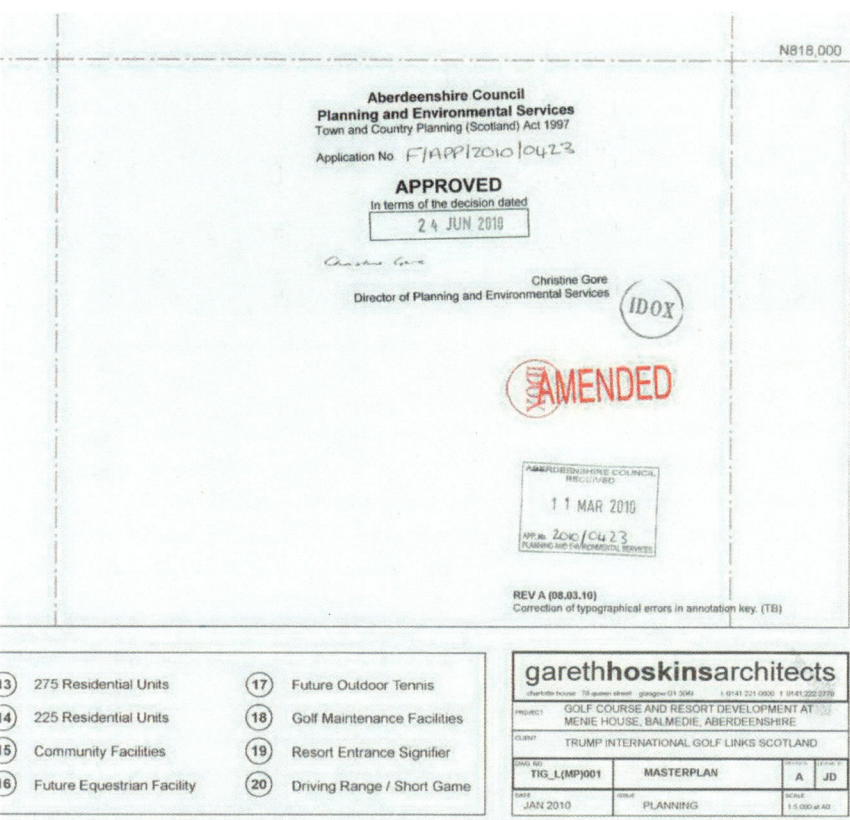

26 May

Donald Trump visits Menie and renames the dunes 'The Great Dunes of Scotland'.

27 May

A horse rider is detained by Trump security following allegations that she has been riding over an area of freshly planted marram grass. The rider describes the situations as follows:

"[I] went for a ride down through the dunes beside the Trump area. Was outside the fences and on the path when they're [sic] security jeep drove down. Carried on back onto the beach and further down, the jeep with flashing orange lights comes powering out of the dunes and storming up the beach towards me – really motoring along, splashing through puddles, lights flashing. Eventually two big fancy blacked-out Range Rovers turn up and four Americans in suits jump out of each one and start accusing me of the vandalism that was in the papers a couple of weeks ago. They were really quite aggressive and if Lenny [my horse] hadn't been freaking out and running round me in circles, it would have really been intimidating."

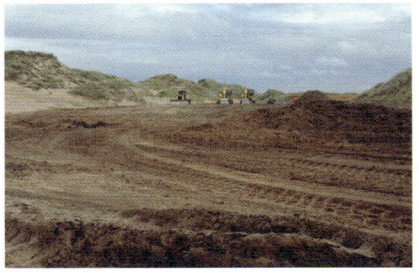 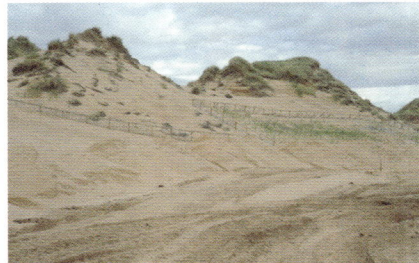

Construction of golf course, August 2010.

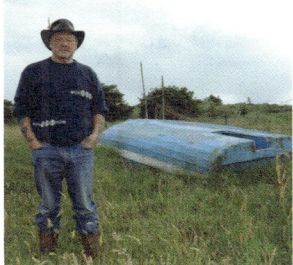

Mike Forbes with his boat on contested land, 2010.

30 June

'APPROVED': full planning permission given for championship golf course.

1 July

Construction officially begins on the golf course.

28 July

Water supply to Mill of Menie is cut off and residents have to collect water from the burn. Mike Forbes makes several calls to TIGLS but nothing is done. The Forbes family is without water for a week.

30 July

Two journalists, Anthony Baxter and Richard Phinney, are arrested at Leyton Cottage, the home of Susan and John Munro, while making the documentary *You've Been Trumped*. Two police officers, PC Wilkinson (No.0728) and PC McKay (No. 0898) tell them to turn the camera off. They are detained under Section 14 of the Criminal Procedure (Scotland) Act 1995.

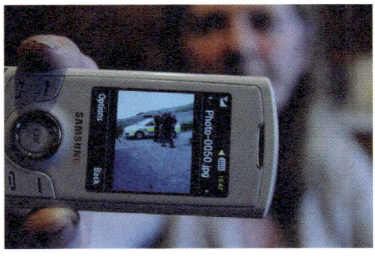

Susan Munro displays a photo on her phone of Ant and Richard's arrest. Leyton Cottage, 30 July 2010.

3 August

Trump construction workers, along with two officers from Grampian Police, remove Mike Forbes's property, including salmon-fishing equipment, from a disputed area of land. Forbes regards the land as belonging to him and is angry. Forbes shows the police his title deeds but the police claim that any dispute is a civil matter and they have no locus. A digger moves onto the site and destroys Forbes' salmon-net drying station and dumps it onto what Trump considers to be his land. These actions, in the presence of police officers, are legally questionable.

4 August

Grampian Police write to Anthony Baxter stating that they have received a report that he was responsible for the crime of breach of the peace at Menie House on 30 July. They state that there is sufficient evidence to report the matter to the procurator fiscal but that on this occasion, they will instead be issuing a written warning. Baxter exercises his right to challenge this and in January 2011, the Crown Office states that it will not be proceeding. All charges are dropped and the police records on Baxter and Phinney are destroyed.

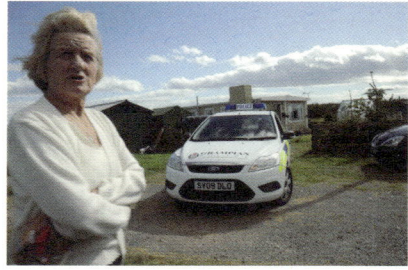

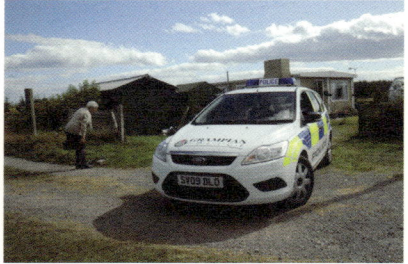

Grampian Police stop Alicia's portrait session with Molly at Mill of Menie, 21 August 2010.

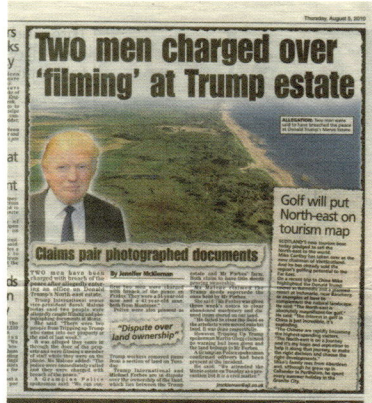

Evening Express, 5 August 2010.

August

Mike Forbes finds red flags on his property, calls the police to report them, and is later charged with theft of the flags. He is on the front page of *Evening Express* same day with the headline 'Trump opponent quizzed by cops'.

21 August

Grampian Police hear via Trump's team that there is 'unusual activity in the area'. A photo shoot is taking place and police request the camera be put away.

12 September

Grampian Police have been called to Menie Estate thirty times since planning permission was granted, responding to various allegations from TIGLS, including vandalism.

Paul Holleran, the National Union of Journalists' organiser in Scotland, says in the *Guardian* that the arrests of Baxter and Phinney were unjustified

and had important implications for press freedom.

"This is a blatant example of police interference aimed at stopping bona fide journalists from doing their job. Their footage shows they were asking very pertinent questions in a mannerly fashion as befits professional journalists. I believe this is a breach of human rights, and we are taking legal advice. I think this must be one of the first court cases in this country of journalists being arrested for just carrying out interviews to establish the truth and hold people to account."

22 September

David Ewen, chief reporter for Aberdeen's *Evening Express*, publishes the book *Chasing Paradise: Donald Trump and the Battle for the World's Greatest Golf Course*.

7 October

Donald Trump, George Sorial, and Donald Trump Jr visit Hermit Point. David Milne asks Trump and his entourage not to come onto his land. Donald Trump is then filmed by the US's Golf Channel touring the golf course with his staff, stopping

in view of Hermit Point. As the staff get out of their vehicles, Trump tells Sarah Malone, his executive vice president, "Sarah, I want to get rid of that house." She replies, "It's going to create a bit of a stir but if we're up for it, let's do it." Trump then says to camera, "There are some houses quite far away from the course, but nevertheless, they are in view. But we are berming some of the areas so that you don't see the houses. I don't want to see the houses ... and nobody has a problem with it … I guess maybe the people that live in the houses have ...".

8 October

Trump receives an honorary degree from Robert Gordon University from local businessmen Sir Ian Wood.

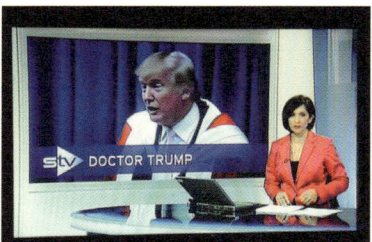

Screenshot: 'Dr Trump' on STV 6 pm News, 8 October 2010.

Chapelfield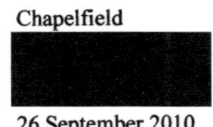

26 September 2010

Acting Principal
The Robert Gordon University
Schoolhill
Aberdeen

Dear Professor Harper

Having recently learnt of the decision to award an honorary degree of the university on Donald Trump, I feel I have no alternative but to return the honorary degree conferred upon me by the university some years ago.

It was always my view that honorary degrees were ideally bestowed upon people who could be readily admired, who could be looked up to as honourable people, and who could serve as role models for students of the university. I well recall the Governing Body rejecting nominations because of considerations of this kind.

Donald Trump fits none of these attributes in my opinion. From what little I have read about him, he claims to be brutal and tough, believing that one cannot be too greedy, and readily boasting of the number of people he has fired. These are not attributes I admire, nor would I wish to see them either cultivated or encouraged among the younger generation. In recent years we have witnessed the consequences of unbridled greed, largely stemming from property development and the marketing of debt as assets. Now, ordinary, innocent people around the world are being made to suffer for such folly.

Much the same is true about the destruction of the natural environment. It is treated as an asset to be owned and exploited no matter the consequences, whether for people or for nature itself. Our world, by which I mean the biosphere, is being rapidly degraded, not least by people like Trump, who derive satisfaction in 'creative destruction', in destroying in order to rebuild in a way more satisfying – and profitable – to them. That is what the development of the Menie Estate is all about, and is done with a cavalier contempt for those that live there and derive their livelihood therefrom.

Lord Acton remarked many years ago that, "power corrupts and absolute power corrupts absolutely". He made this comment in the context of the proposed dogma of 'papal infallibility', but it seems to have a general validity. Power, which often springs from great wealth, has a corrosive effect that reveals itself in arrogance and a lack of concern for the well being of others. All that matters is the goal, the target, and winning, irrespective of who gets hurt in the process. These are not qualities that I admire, nor would I wish to be associated with them.

No doubt, great thought has been given by the Academic Council and the Governing Body of the honour to be given to Donald Trump. They have exercised their judgement as is their right, but, similarly, after careful consideration I am exercising my right and now return the honorary degree that was conferred upon me and with which I no longer wish to be associated.

Yours sincerely

David A Kennedy

8 October

"I don't approve of bullying": Ex-principal of Robert Gordon University David Kennedy gives back his honorary doctorate in protest of Trump's honorary doctorate.

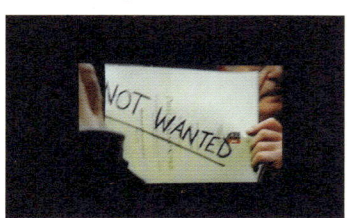

Screenshot: 'NOT WANTED', David Kennedy, on STV 6 pm News, 8 October 2010.

9 October

The March Of Menie.

12 October

Dundas & Wilson, the law firm acting for TIGLS, writes the following to the Milnes: "Our clients, Trump International Golf Club Scotland Limited, have advised us that you currently have a fence and part of a shed (or other building) erected on land belonging to them. Please note that our clients now intend to remove the fence. They may, at their sole option, re-erect the fence along the legal boundary of your property as shown on the attached plan. No further notice will be issued to you in this respect. With regard to the shed, our clients require you to remove the part of the shed that is on their land within 72 hours, failing which they reserve their right to raise an action in the Sheriff Court for removal."

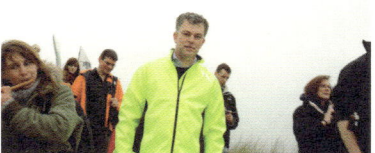

Councillor Martin Ford at the March of Menie.

18 October

TIGLS contractors arrive at Hermit Point and erect a new fence along the drive and around the Milnes' property.

October

20-foot bunds of earth built in front of Leyton Cottage. Donald Trump, speaking to course designers about the location of a tee on 7 October 2010 and looking towards the Munros' house, says, "I would give this some extra curve so that you're hitting that way ... OK? You're not hitting at the houses, you're hitting that way. Now, that house is going to be gone because you're putting a big dune right there ... all right? This is fantastic?"

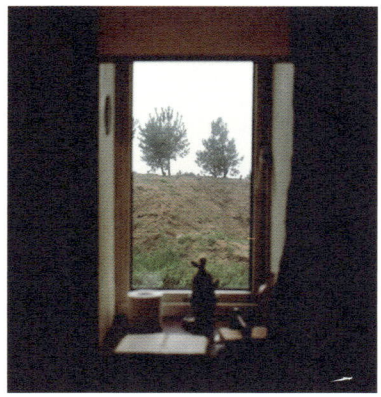

View from upstairs windows at Leyton Cottage showing the mountains of earth and trees planted by Trump to hide the home and block the view.

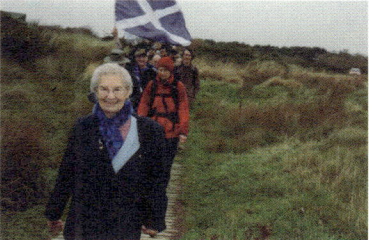

Molly Forbes leads the March of Menie.

21 October

Paul O'Connor is fired by Trump after refusing to be part of a 'campaign of intimidation'.

28 October

Molly Forbes loses the final round of her legal challenge to Trump. Judge rules she must pay Trump's five-figure legal costs.

21 December

TIGLS sends the Milnes a letter and invoice for £2,820 for a boundary fence Trump has had erected around the Milnes' home.

The *Press and Journal*, Thursday, 28 October 2010.

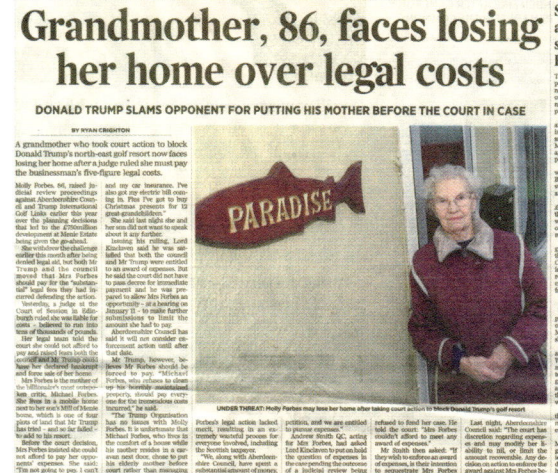

Grandmother, 86, faces losing her home over legal costs

DONALD TRUMP SLAMS OPPONENT FOR PUTTING HIS MOTHER BEFORE THE COURT IN CASE

2011

14 January
Alicia's *Menie: a portrait of a North East coastal community in conflict* exhibition opens at Peacock Visual Arts, Aberdeen.

30 January
TIGLS announces that it will no longer be pursuing CPOs.

February
National Galleries of Scotland acquire Alicia's portraits *Mike & Sheila Forbes: Mill of Menie* and *Molly Forbes: Paradise.*

March
TIGLS imports four-meter-tall Sitka spruce trees and begins to plant them around the boundaries of the Milnes' house, blocking light and views.

5 June
Another March of Menie.

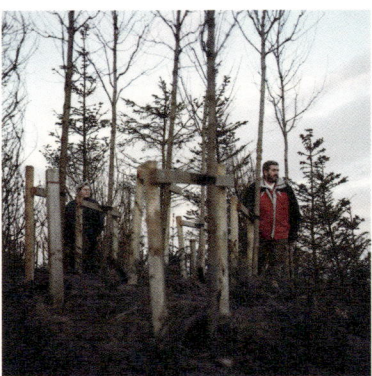

David and Moira Milne inspect trees planted around their home, Hermit Point, Sunday, 27 January 2013.

11 June
First Minister Alex Salmond responds to David Milne's letter of concern, justifying his decision-making regarding Trump and the construction of his golf course.

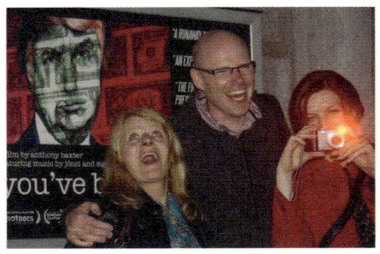

Susan Munro, Anthony Baxter, and Alicia Bruce at the premiere of *You've Been Trumped.*

17 June 2011
Documentary *You've Been Trumped* director Anthony Baxter has a Green Carpet premiere at the Belmont Cinema, Aberdeen, accompanied by an exhibition of Alicia's photographs.

2012

9 February
Trump writes to Alex Salmond accusing the First Minister of seeming "hell bent on destroying Scotland's coastline".

March
Donald Trump Does Bohemian Rhapsody film, featuring a puppet Trump, is launched on YouTube, receiving 30,000 hits in two days and is about to go viral when it is taken down by YouTube and all other sites across the internet.

23 April
Karine Polwart performs the song 'Cover Your Eyes' at a special screening of *You've Been Trumped* at the Scottish Parliament.

24 April
Donald Trump tells MSPs "I am the evidence" at a Scottish Parliament committee meeting whilst challenging future Scottish government proposals for wind-farm development.

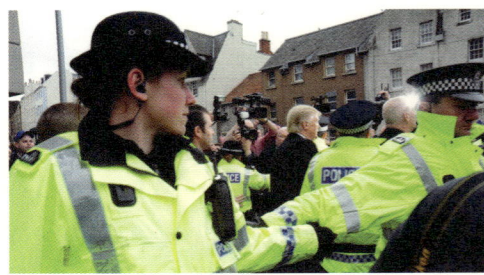

Donald Trump leaves Scottish Parliament amid protests and media scrum, 24 April 2012.

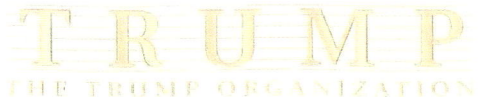
February 9, 2012

Dear First Minister Salmond:

I have read your recent statements concerning so called "wind power." For the record, taxing your citizens to subsidize wind projects owned by foreign energy companies will destroy your country and its economy. Jobs will not be created in Scotland because these ugly monstrosities known as turbines are manufactured in other countries such as China. These countries, who so benefit from your billions of pounds in payments, are laughing at you!

After years of wasteful spending, several members of the European Union, such as Holland, have already abandoned their offshore wind power programs because they have failed and because these horrendous machines are destroying the beauty of their countries. Perhaps the reason these turbines are referred to as "renewable" is because every five years they need to be replaced with new equipment, or renewed - - - the salt water and harsh conditions rapidly erode these structures. Who is going to pay for the new installations then? Not you, for you will be long gone, but the people of Scotland will forever suffer! With the reckless installation of these monsters, you will single-handedly have done more damage to Scotland than virtually any event in Scottish history!

You seem hell bent on destroying Scotland's coastline and therefore, Scotland itself - - - but I will never be "on board," as you have stated I would be, with this insanity. As a matter of fact, I have just authorized my staff to allocate a substantial amount of money to launch an international campaign to fight your plan to surround Scotland's coast with many thousands of wind turbines - - - it will be like looking through the bars of a prison and the Scottish citizens will be the prisoners! Luckily, tourists will not suffer because there will be none as they will be going to other countries that had the foresight to use other forms of energy. In fact, I understand that other European leaders, including those of Ireland in particular, are almost as happy as the turbine manufacturers themselves by what you are doing - - - they will be taking all of your tourism and business.

Please understand that I am doing this to save Scotland and honour my mother, Mary MacLeod who, as you know, was born and raised in Stornoway. She would not believe what you are doing to her beloved Scotland!

Yours sincerely,

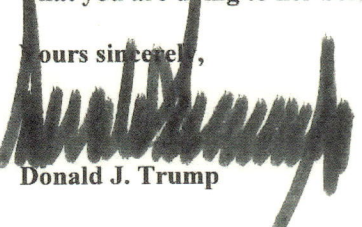

Donald J. Trump

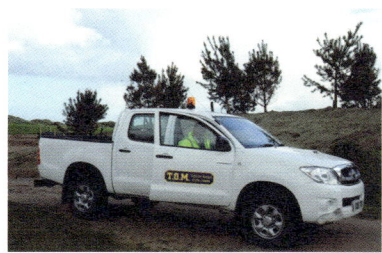

Trump security threatens Alicia.

3 June

Trump security guard threatens to smash Alicia's camera. Grampian Police issue the guard a Formal Adult Warning.

July

Scottish Wildlife Trust send an open letter to golfers urging them not to play Trump's course.

10 July

Trump International Golf Links Scotland is officially opened by golfer Colin Montgomerie.

24 October

Trump offers President Barack Obama $5 million if he can show his birth certificate.

October

Walker Hilary Nicol discovers gorse planted near the boundaries of the golf course, blocking the right to roam.

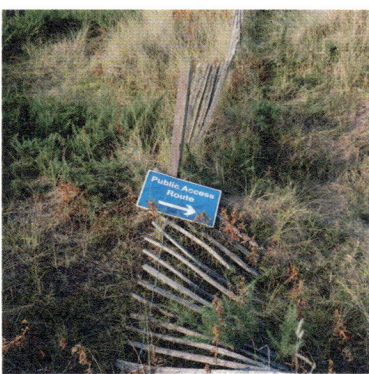

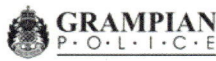

GRAMPIAN
P·O·L·I·C·E

Keeping our communities safe

Grampian Police
Bridge Street
Ellon
AB41 9AX

Our Ref: S/CR/18/F309/8230/SD/12
Your Ref:

Tel: 0845 600-5-700
Fax: 01224 304220
ServiceCentre@grampian.pnn.police.uk
www.grampian.police.uk

Date: 8 June 2012

Alicia Bruce

Dear Ms Bruce

CRIMEFILE REFERENCE 0207770612

I am sorry to hear that you were the victim of Threatening or Abusive Behaviour at Leyton Cottages, Balmedie on 3 June 2012.

Whilst this must have been a very distressing experience for you, I am pleased to inform you that the crime has been detected and, having considered the circumstances, the person responsible for the crime has received a formal Police Warning.

This Warning will be recorded formally on the Scottish Criminal History System Database where it will remain for a period of two years, during which time the information will be available to all Police Forces.

In the meantime, I trust that this information is of assistance to you.

Yours sincerely

Steve Pratt
Inspector

3 November

The annual Menie bonfire and fireworks hosted by the Forbes family.

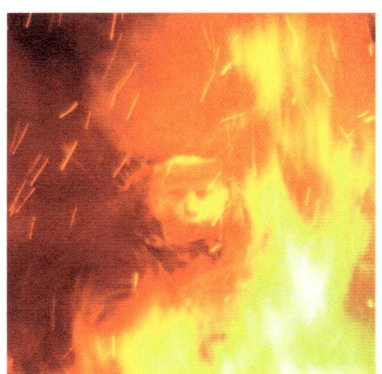

10 November

Daily Mail run article about Trump security threatening Alicia.

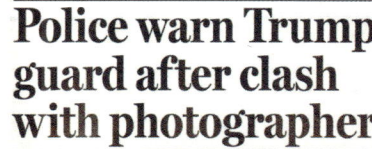

Police warn Trump guard after clash with photographer

By Jonathan Brocklebank

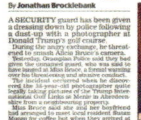
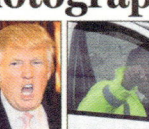
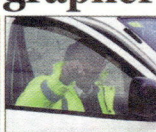
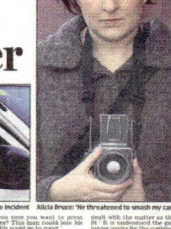

30 November

Mike Forbes wins 'Top Scot' at Glenfiddich Spirit of Scotland Awards, voted on by the public.

5 December

Trump bans Glenfiddich whisky from all of his venues and gives himself an award.

2013

January

Writer Suzanne Kelly documents the golf course collapsing near Balmedie beach and publishes a story in *Aberdeen Voice*.

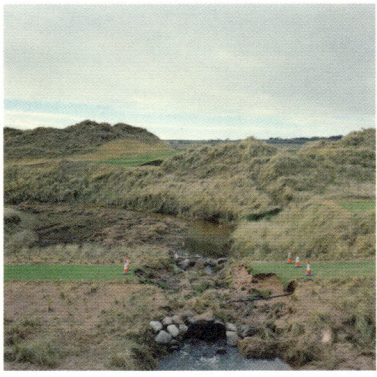

Collapsed golf course, 27 January 2013; Alicia Bruce.

18 February

Scottish Parliament's exhibition of Menie takes place during Scotland's Climate Week.

Alicia's Menie project celebrated in Parliamentary Motion S4M-05749.

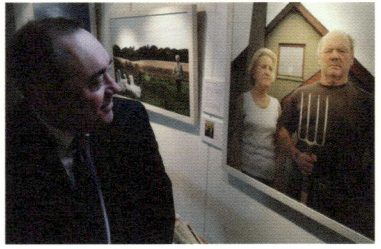

First Minister Alex Salmond arranges to meet with Mike Forbes following his conversation with Alicia at the Scottish Parliament.

21 February

First Minister Alex Salmond talks to Alicia about the exhibition and admits that, in spite of the Forbes family being his constituents, he has never been to their houses. He claims he was misrepresented in *You've Been Trumped* and that he has distanced himself from Trump, but in terms of the development, "the economic benefits far outweigh the environmental impact". He offers the photographer the chance to be photographed with him. She asks for a picture of him looking Mike and Sheila in the eye.

21 February

First Minister Alex Salmond arranges to meet with Mike Forbes the day after his conversation with Alicia.

27 February

Alicia Bruce's Menie project is celebrated in a parliamentary motion.

18 April

The tables turn as local press start to disagree with Trump.

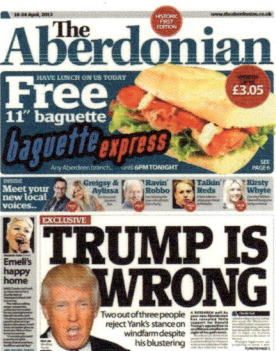

Motion S4M-05749: Patrick Harvie, Glasgow, Scottish Green Party, Date Lodged: 27/02/2013
Menie Community Photography Project
That the Parliament congratulates the award-winning Aberdeenshire photographer, Alicia Bruce, on her ongoing photography project about Menie, an area of outstanding natural beauty on the Aberdeenshire coast; understands that her photographs from this series have gained international acclaim and have been published in *The Times*, *The Scotsman* and several arts magazines, and that two of the portraits have been acquired by the National Galleries of Scotland, and welcomes that Alicia's photographs, many of which restage compositions from celebrated paintings, have helped to tell the story of the residents of Menie, whose homes came under threat due to what it considers the bullish golf course development of Donald Trump, and to portray a side of that story that otherwise might have gone unheard.

Supported by: Alison Johnstone, David Stewart, Jean Urquhart, Neil Findlay, Jackie Baillie, Richard Lyle, Colin Beattie, Nigel Don, Malcolm Chisholm

Top Scot Forbes makes a spirited return

Trump's nemesis back after 38 years

BRIAN FERGUSON
ARTS CORRESPONDENT

THE last time Michael Forbes visited Edinburgh was 38 years ago, when he arrived at Leith Docks on a fishing trawler.

That probably only partly explained the look of bewilderment on his face as he took to the stage – in full Highland dress – to collect the "Top Scot" honour to a hero's standing ovation at the Prestonfield Hotel in Edinburgh.

The success of Mr Forbes – the 60-year-old nemesis of tycoon Donald Trump – in claiming top honour in the Glenfiddich Spirit of Scotland awards sparked a torrent of late-night tributes on Twitter, to which he was also oblivious as he fended off a flood of congratulations at the ceremony.

> "I've no idea what Trump will make of the award"
> *Michael Forbes*

His brief "I'm speechless" address from the stage was the only hint of disappointment at the 15th annual event, which saw the acclaim for Mr Forbes topped only by the reception for Scotland's Olympic and Paralympic heroes.

Presented with the award by a previous Olympic idol, sailing star Shirley Robertson, they were represented by Olympic canoeing champion Tim Baillie, Paralympic cyclist Neil Fachie and Paralympic rower David Smith. They accepted the award on behalf of a total of nine London heroes, who also included equestrian winner Scott Brash, rower Katherine Grainger, cycling icon Sir Chris Hoy, tennis star Andy Murray, rower Heather Stanning, and cyclist Craig MacLean.

Baillie said it had been an "absolute privilege" for the athletes to accept the award, particularly after the backing that they had received in London over the summer. "It's quite nice that the judges chose not to split the award. It would have been very hard to try to choose between all the achievements we all saw in Britain over the summer.

"I'd like to thank the public for their support as it would not have been as special without a home crowd. It was a huge opportunity and platform in London, and also to come back for the homecoming parade in Glasgow."

The 15th annual ceremony, set by the whisky brand in partnership with *The Scotsman* to recognise "inspirational individuals" across a wide cultural spectrum, saw seven other awards handed out.

If the London Games were the undisputed sporting highlight of the year for Scotland, then it was the Disney-Pixar film *Brave* which was the big cultural winner, helping to land the screen honour for Kelly Macdonald, who played the lead role of rebellious princess Merida, and North Uist singer Julie Fowlis, the main star of the soundtrack.

Fowlis, a torchbearer for Gaelic song for well over a decade now, won the public poll up against strong competition from Emili Sande, violinist Nicola Benedetti and indie favourite Johnny Lynch, better known as Fence Collective favourite Pictish Trail.

In the absence of Macdonald, Leslie Hills, the festival's outgoing chair, read a message from the Glaswegian star, saying: "I'm very honoured. I was really lucky to be part of a production with so many other Scottish artists and a film that portrays our country so well."

If Fowlis and Macdonald are well established household names, the winner of the art award recognised a figure who has remained elusively in the shadows, despite being the key figure behind the critically acclaimed new Fringe venue Summerhall over the last two summers.

In a brief speech, Robert McDowell, who bought the former Royal Dick vet school building from Edinburgh University for several million pounds, said: "It is a new, huge, mad thing that we are doing there, but it is the spirit of Richard Demarco, it is the spirit of the Edinburgh Festival I hope it will grow and express the spirit of all the arts."

Gustavo Pardo, the founder of the Edinburgh-based coffee emporium Artisan Roast, which is now recognised as the best cafe in the UK, won the food category.

He said: "It was only a few years ago before we set up that it was so difficult to get a decent coffee in Edinburgh, but it is now seen as one of the capital cities of coffee anywhere in the UK."

Glaswegian author Ewan Morrison published two books in 2012 and it about to see another, *Swung*, turned into a big-screen film, said he was pleased that his work had been recognised with the writing prize in the face of the "dumbing down" of literature and paid tribute to the backing he had received from the "much-maligned" Creative Scotland.

The other two awards saw the charity Trees for Life's founder Alan Watson Featherstone recognised in the environment category while Lucina Bruce-Gardyne, the creator of a gluten-free bread, won the business honour.

As for Mr Forbes – who will now be invited back to attend future Spirit of Scotland award ceremonies – the Top Scot was left to speculate on the reaction of Donald Trump.

"I actually thought the award should have gone to Anthony Baxter, who made the documentary. I've no idea what Donald Trump will make of the award. I'm sure he'll have something to say about it at some point."

From left clockwise, Gaelic singer Julie Fowlis, Olympic sailor Shirley Robertson, Lady Claire Macdonald and Lord Godfrey McDonald, Michael Forbes with his Top Scot trophy, Kirsty Wark, Robert McDowell being congratulated by Richard Demarco, and in the centre environmental winner Alan Watson Featherson is presented with his award by Lesley Riddoch
Pictures: Phil Wilkinson

GERRY HASSAN
Why Menie battle could be beacon for communities
PAGE 26

Trump film-maker reveals plan for sequel

BRIAN FERGUSON

THE film-maker behind the award-winning documentary about Donald Trump's golf course development in Aberdeenshire has revealed he has begun work on a follow-up.

Anthony Baxter said he had started shooting what he described as a "sequel" to *You've Been Trumped*, which showed Michael Forbes' tussles with the tycoon over his refusal to sell-up and make way for the £750 million development.

Mr Baxter said he intends to have the next film finished in time for the Scottish

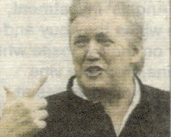
Donald Trump provides the inspiration for another film

independence referendum, and will explore the political fall-out from the Menie development, examine progress on the other elements of the project which have yet to get off the ground and look at other "horrific" golf course developments around the world.

Mr Baxter has won funding in the form of a £10,000 grant from Creative Scotland, to help distribute and promote *You've Been Trumped* around the world, having initially been turned down by the agency, BBC Scotland and the Edinburgh International Film Festival.

The documentary was eventually screened at the Toronto Film Festival after being rejected for Scotland's flagship cinematic showcase.

2014

24 June

Menie residents and Ant Baxter attend the premiere of Baxter's documentary *A Dangerous Game* at Edinburgh International Film Festival.

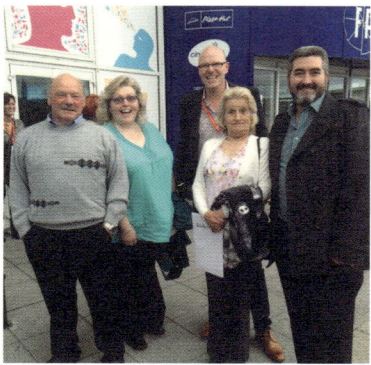

Mike, Moira, Sheila, and David attend the premiere with director Ant Baxter.

18 September

Referendum vote takes place in Scotland.

19 September

Results announced: 55.3% vote 'No' and 44.7% vote 'Yes' for Scottish independence.

2015

5 June

Scottish Courts and Tribunals: Trump International Golf Club Scotland Limited and the Trump Organization LLC against the Scottish Ministers over construction of wind farms.

16 June

Donald Trump announces US presidential campaign.

16 December

Donald Trump loses Supreme Court battle to block wind farms in view of his Scottish golf resort.

"History will judge those involved unfavourably and the outcome demonstrates the foolish, small-minded and parochial mentality which dominates the current Scottish Government's dangerous experiment with wind energy," says Trump's spokesman.

2016

5 April

Rohan Beyts is charged under the Criminal Procedure (Scotland) Act, having been followed and filmed urinating in the sand dunes by three men: two employees of Trump and a newspaper photographer.

21 June

Menie residents David Milne and Mike Forbes raise Mexican flags on their land in a symbolic reminder of those Trump has offended locally and internationally.

24 June

Trump Turnberry opens. Scottish comedian Janey Godley protests on-site with a placard that says 'Trump Is a Cunt'.

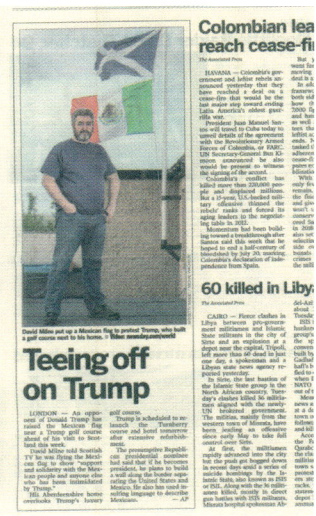

19 July

Trump becomes the official Republican US presidential nominee.

9 November

Trump wins the US presidential election.

2017

20 January

Trump is inaugurated as 45th President of the United States.

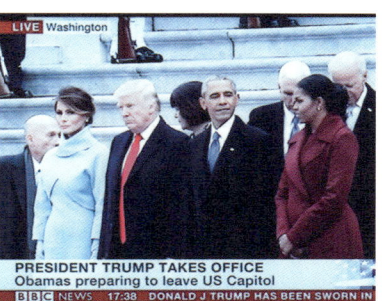

2018

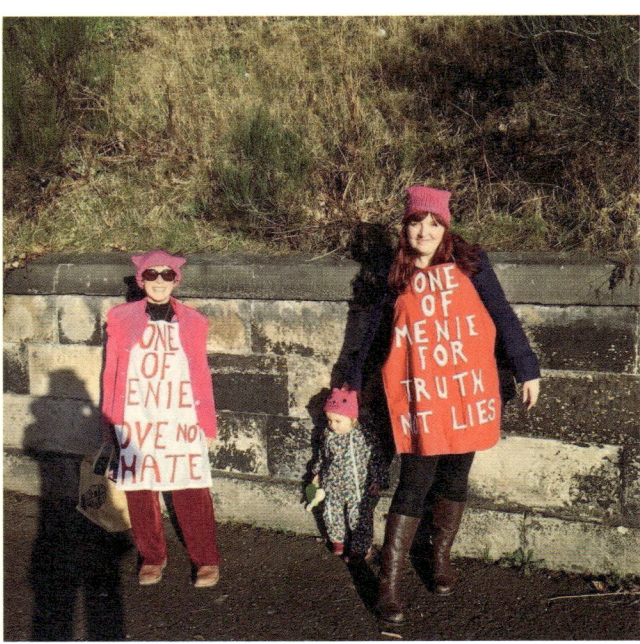

21 January 2017 Women's March in Edinburgh. Rohan Beyts, Alicia Bruce, and Alicia's daughter attend.

2 March

Mickey Foote, Menie resident and producer of the Clash's first album dies at the age of 66.

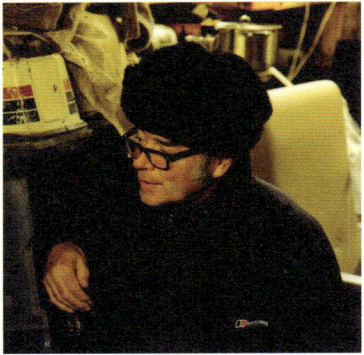

Mickey Foote at a party in Mike Forbes's barn, Mill of Menie, 2012.

2019

21 January

The Women's March takes place as a response to Trump's inauguration the day before. It is a global protest against Trump's rhetoric, misogyny, and the threat he poses to women's rights. Rohan Beyts speaks publicly at the event of being followed by Trump security and her court case at the Edinburgh march. Alicia attends with her one-year-old daughter. The aprons the women wore are now in the collection of the Glasgow Women's Library.

25 January

Trump signs an executive order directing the Department of Homeland Security to construct a wall along the Mexico-U.S. border.

5 March

Former Eurythmics singer Annie Lennox speaks at a rally before International Women's Day. She says Trump's 'locker room talk' is a catalyst for action and that the election of the billionaire has energised the push for women's rights. Lennox grew up in Aberdeen.

April

Rohan Beyts loses her court case against TIGLS on a technicality, but the sheriff is critical of Trump Org.

25 January

The government watchdog Scottish Natural Heritage recommends that Site of Special Scientific Interest (SSSI) accreditation be removed from Menie links.

October

Trump's Aberdeenshire golf resort posts £1m in annual losses.

13 November

Trump is forced to pay £225,000 to the Scottish government after losing the fight over a wind farm.

Obituaries

Molly Forbes

Ordinary Scot who became known worldwide as Donald Trump's nemesis

Molly Forbes, smallholder. Born: 20 April 1924 in Whitecairns. Died: 11 April 2021 in Aberdeen, aged 96

Molly Forbes would not have expected her obituary to appear in a national newspaper. A retired caterer, a mother, grandmother and great-grandmother, she enjoyed living quietly on her son's land in Aberdeenshire – until their way of life came under threat from one of the most powerful men in the world.

Molly and her neighbours found themselves cast as the unlikely opponents of Donald Trump when he tried to have them evicted from their land at Menie, north of Aberdeen, to make room for his luxury golf resort. During the development, Trump had a wall built around their property so that visitors to the resort would not have to see them, and Molly and her family lived for five years without a reliable water supply.

As events at Menie attracted international news coverage, Molly's quiet determination and dignity shone out, reminding the world that they never intended to be activists but were simply people who wanted to be treated with respect and left in peace. In retrospect, the Menie folk were among the first to experience bullying tactics the rest of the world would come to recognise.

Mary Buchan Lamb was born on a farm at Whitecairns, a few miles from Menie, in 1924, the daughter of James Lamb, a crofter, contractor and ploughman, and Annie, his wife. She had two sisters, Nancy and Annie. She treasured grainy black and white film footage of her father working his plough, playing his fiddle and singing traditional ballads.

Educated at Craigie School, Whitecairns, she worked as a land girl during the Second World War. She would later tell filmmaker Anthony Baxter, maker of the award-winning You've Been Trumped (2011) and the sequel You've Been Trumped Too (2016), about looking after a dairy herd of 30 cows and singing to them as they were milked.

In 1948, she wed Walter Forbes – Wattie – who spent much of his life at sea, first as a salmon fisherman, then working on a fisheries research boat. They had seven children: Walter, Noreen, Evelyn, Lorna, Michael, Sylvia and Shereen.

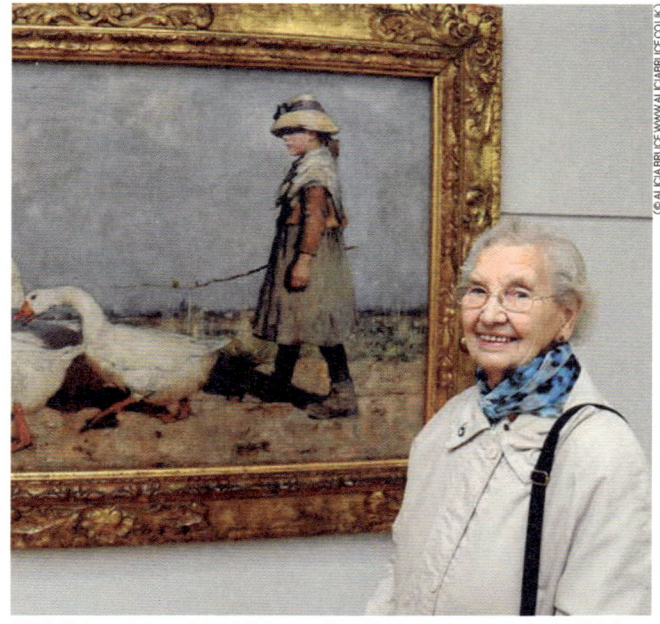

↑ Molly Forbes with James Guthrie's To Pastures New, which inspired a portrait of her by Alicia Bruce

(© ALICIA BRUCE WWW.ALICIABRUCE.CO.UK)

After working for a time as a hospital cleaner in Aberdeen, Molly became a waitress in the canteen at Grampian Television, and liked to tell stories about serving meals for the station's stars. She later worked in catering, including at the Beechgrove Garden where the popular TV show was made.

After Walter's death in 1999, when she felt the area of Aberdeen in which she lived was changing for the worse, she moved to a chalet on the smallholding of her son Mike at Menie, where she enjoyed the rural environment, keeping hens and geese. She called her home Paradise, and loved to welcome guests, including her numerous grandchildren and great grandchildren.

Everything changed in 2006 when Donald Trump, then best known as a New York property developer and the host of US version of The Apprentice, bought the 1,400-acre Menie estate, boasting that he would build "the world's best golf course", along with a 450-room luxury hotel, 36 golf villas, 950 holiday homes and 500 houses, and would bring 6,000 jobs to the area.

The proposal was rejected by an Aberdeenshire Council planning committee, partly because ancient sand dunes on the site were a recognised Site of Special Scientific Interest (SSSI), but this was overturned by an inquiry ordered by the Scottish Government in 2008. The following year, the Trump Organization asked Aberdeenshire Council to use its powers of compulsory purchase to acquire additional land, including that of Molly's family and her neighbours, something he later denied. This led to the Tripping Up Trump campaign, which drew many supporters to the area and gave the Menie cause nationwide publicity.

When work began on the site, contractors building a road damaged a pipe carrying water from a spring on Trump land to supply the Forbes' homes. For much the next five years, their water supply was cut off or contaminated, leaving Molly, then in her late 80s, using a wheelbarrow and paint pots to carry water from a stream for her livestock and garden, and needing bottled water to drink and cook with.

Trump hurled insults at the Forbes, describing their home as "a pigsty". However, dignity and common sense to the fore, Molly described Trump as "a bairn who has never grown up". The golf course and a 19-room hotel opened in 2012; it still has fewer than 100 employees. The 4,000-year-old sand dunes have been partially destroyed and lost their SSSI status last year.

Molly said: "All this attention makes me feel like a celebrity and I'm nae. I'm just an ordinary person. I live in Paradise, my home in Menie, but it's feeling less like Paradise these days." When Trump told media that Molly reminded him of his own mother, she said she hoped he had treated his own mother better than he treated her. She received letters of support from all over the world, all of which she tried to answer personally.

Photographer Alicia Bruce created a series of portraits of the residents, "Menie: Trumped", each inspired by a classic painting. Offered a selection of paintings to choose from, Molly opted for James Guthrie's To Pastures New, a painting of a young girl herding geese which she felt chimed with her optimistic outlook.

The photograph, which took some hours to create, and was even interrupted by a visit from the police after the Trump organisation reported "unusual activity" at the smallholding, is now in the collection of the Scottish National Portrait Gallery. It also hung in Molly's living room for the rest of her life at Menie, and went with her to the care home where she spent her final months.

SUSAN MANSFIELD

2020

5 February
Trump is impeached.

23 April
There is an outcry after Trump suggests injecting disinfectant as a treatment for Covid-19.

12 September
Sheila Forbes (1947–2020) dies suddenly at home at the age of 73.

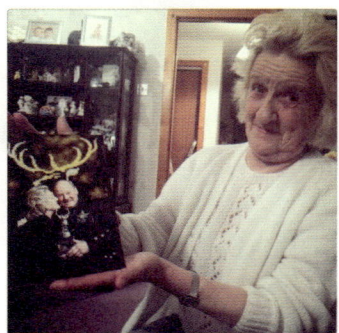

Sheila Forbes, 2012.

October 2020
Construction of a second Trump golf course at Menie is approved.

9 December
Loss of SSSI accreditation, per NatureScot:
"Parts of the dunes on Foveran Links have lost their status as a nationally important protected wildlife site, after consideration of the scientific evidence by the Protected Areas Committee (PAC) of NatureScot. The PAC concluded that, following construction of the Trump International Golf Links course on the dune system at Menie Estate, this area no longer merits being retained as part of the Site of Special Scientific Interest (SSSI)."

29 December
Susan Munro (1953–2020) passes away after a long illness, at the age of 67.

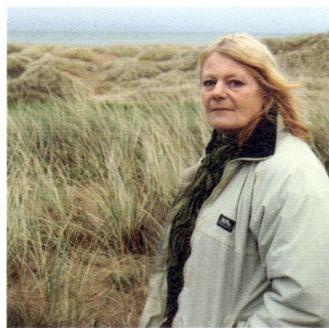

Susan Munro, 2012.

2021

6 January
Trump supporters storm the US Capitol. The attack is part of a seven-part plan by Trump to overturn the election. Five people die in the riot.

13 January
Trump is impeached for a second time, one week before his presidency ends.

11 April
Molly Forbes (1924–2021), smallholder and Trump opposer, passes away at the age of 96.

11 September
There is a small ceremony to mark one year since Sheila Forbes' death. Her husband Mike, a quarryman and salmon fisherman, has built her cairn with granite, the stone which Aberdeen, the Granite City is famed for. The cairn displays a photograph of the couple when they were young.

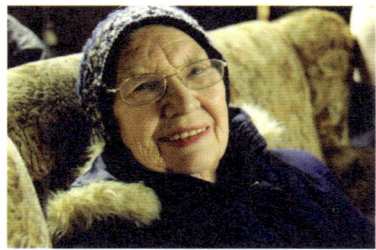

Molly Forbes, 2012.

2022   2023

10 July

Local resident discovers that the 'T' is missing from 'Trump International Golf Links Scotland' on the ten-year anniversary of the courses official opening.

February

Construction starts on a second Trump golf course and housing in Menie, designed to swallow up the remaining sand dunes all the way to Balmedie Country Park.

14 July

Ivana, Donald Trump's first wife and the mother of his children, is found dead after falling in her Manhattan home. She is buried at Trump National Golf Club Bedminster. According to New Jersey state tax laws, land that is used as a cemetery is exempt from all taxes, rates, and assessments.

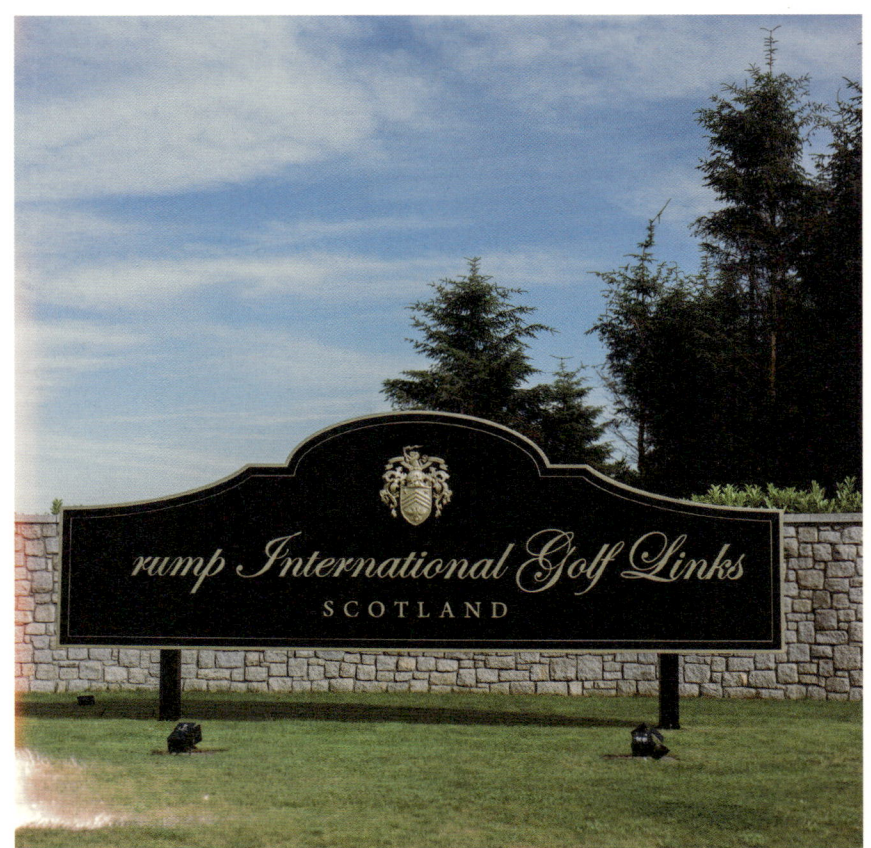

Trump International Golf Links Scotland, 10 July 2022. The 'T' is missing from Trump's sign on what is also the ten-year anniversary of the course opening.

ACKNOWLEDGMENTS

For Andrew and Scarlet Rafferty

In memory of
Sheila Forbes, Molly Forbes, Mickey Foote, and Susan Munro

A tribute to my friends, the Menie residents
Mike Forbes, Sheila Forbes, Molly Forbes, Susan Munro, John Munro, Moira Milne, David Milne, Mickey Foote, Kym Swindells, Val Banks, and their extended families

With love and thanks to

Writers
Dr Catriona McAra
Karine Polwart
Lesley Riddoch
Louise Pearson

Contribution of research
Andy Wightman, 'Donald Trump's Ego Trip', 2011

Editorial support
Eleanor Thom

Trace Mentorship Program
Cindy Sissokho
Emma Bowkett
Fiona Rogers
Haley Morris Cafiero
Sebah Chaudhry
Sian Bonnell

Daylight team
Ursula Damm
Gabi Fastman
Michael Itkoff

Providers of supportive quotes for the Kickstarter
Ben Harman, Director of Stills, Edinburgh
Christiane Monarchi, *Photomonitor*
Malcolm Dickson, Director of Street Level Photoworks, Glasgow
Nicky Bird, Glasgow School of Art

Musicians who generously donated gigs to the Kickstarter
Karine Polwart
Kathryn Joseph
Ballboy aka Gordon McIntyre

Funding for this book was made possible via a Kickstarter fundraiser in July 2022 where over £22,000 was raised in less than one month.

Thank you to all 340 backers who supported the Kickstarter. The following are Kickstarter backers who chose 'Your Name in the Book'; others wish to remain anonymous or did not select this pledge. I'm thankful to each and every one of you for the love, faith, and solidarity in the making of this book. It was a leap of faith which was made a reality thanks to you.

Adam Rafferty
Alexander Bruce
Alexis Stanislaus
Alistair Brown
Alistair Scott
Alan Rafferty
Andrew Rafferty
Andy Thorn
Angus MacDonald
Ann Landels
Anne Eardley
Annie Lyden
Anneliese Dodds
Becca Freeden
Becky Rafferty
Beverley Hood
Bruce Sutherland
Cal MacAninch
Calum Colvin
Carla Tiffney
Carol Croft
Caryn "CC" Cross
Catherine Abbott
Catherine Spencer
Catriona Grant
Celine Marchbank
Charlotte Hale
Ciara Leeming
Claire Craig
Clare Henry
Clare Mackavoy
Colin MacLeod
Colin Thom
David Eustace
David Fulton
David McCue
David Pollock
David Stevenson

David Williams
Debbie Dryburgh
Debbie Swift
Donald Stewart
Duckrabbit
Edward Brydon
Emily Jane Porter
Ewan Willison
Fiona Clark
Finlay Matheson
Frances Scott
Gina Ford
Gordon Millar
Gwen Riley Jones
Hannah Ashwell
Helen Trompeteler
Henry Cheese
Howard Woolfson
Iain Irving
Iain Stewart
Ilisa Stack
Jakki Hanlon
Jaskirt Dhaliwal-Boora
Jean West
Jeanette Baratta
Jennifer Blacklaw
Jenny Brownrigg
Jenny Capon
Jenny Messer
Jessica McDermott
Jim Mennie
Joan Rafferty
Joanne Cross
Jocelyn Allen
John Keenan
John Picken
John Gabriel Summers
Joyce W Cairns RSA

Juliana Capes Muir
Julia Taudevin
June Dougherty
Justin Kenrick
Katey McPherson
Katherine Keil
Kenneth Gray
Kerry Curl
Kerry Harker
Laura McWilliam
Laura Noble
Lesley Orr
Lisa Donald
Lorenzo Dutto
Lorraine Grant
Louisa Stratton
Lucy Hackney
Luke Watson
Lydia Goldblatt
Lynn Jamieson
M Masson
Makiko Konishi
Malcolm Dickson
Maria Falconer
Marie-Anne McQuay
Marjolaine Ryley
Mark Cousins
Maro Mcnab
Martin Parr
Meghan Walter
Matthew Sillars
Mhairi Bell-Moodie
Michael Marten
Michael Messmer
Mike Fuller
Moy MacKay
Neil Drysdale
Neil McGuire

Niall McDiarmid
Nicky Bird
Nikola Smith
Normand Rajotte
Olga Wojtas
Oluwatosin Daniju
Otto Lussen
Patricia Macdonald
Peter Gedge
Phillip Bruno
Rachael Cloughton
Rachel Nordstrom
Raphael Swift
Rebecca Macaulay
Rob Menlove
Robin Gillanders
Rosanna Hawthorne
Roxana Allison
Roy Keil
Ruth Barrie
Sarah Saunders
Sharon Thornton
Sheila Masson
Sheila McKinnon
Shirley Barr
Stan Blackley
Stephen Boyd
Sue Edwards
Susan A. Barnett
Susan Mowatt
Suzanne Kelly
Tracy Marshall-Grant
Tripping Up Trump
Valerie Hawthorne
Valerie Page
Victoria Crowe RSA
Vicky Sitton
William Rafferty

All organisations that have supported this project over the years with exhibition space, facilities access, and/or funding, but particularly the following:

Aberdeen City Council
Fix Photo Festival, London
National Galleries of Scotland
Peacock Visual Arts, Aberdeen, Scotland
Street Level Photoworks, Glasgow, Scotland
St Andrews Photo Festival
The Richard and Siobhán Coward Foundation
The Royal Scottish Academy
University of St Andrews Special Collections
Vu Photo, Quebec

Thanks also to every person, newspaper, and organisation who shared the Kickstarter and encouraged others to back the project. I fear I'll miss so many of you if I attempt to do individual thanks; such was the extent of sharing. I am grateful to everyone listed above and all of the anonymous donors, many of whom preordered a book or bought a print; this book is happening because of you. Thank you for helping solidify a history of a remarkable, resilient Scottish community in book format. This is for all of you, too.

BIOS

Alicia Bruce is an award-winning working-class photographer, community collaborator, educator, and activist based in Scotland. Her photography sits between documentary and staged imagery focusing on communities, environments, and human rights. Alicia's photographs are held in several public collections including the National Galleries of Scotland, the University of St Andrews, the Royal Scottish Academy, and the UK Parliament. She is a teaching fellow and tutor at Edinburgh College of Art, The University of Edinburgh. In 2014 Alicia received the prestigious Royal Scottish Academy Morton Award. In 2023 she appeared in the BBC documentary *The Women Who Changed Modern Scotland*.

www.aliciabruce.co.uk

Louise Pearson is a curator of photography at the National Galleries of Scotland. She was recently awarded an Art Fund grant to increase diversity in the National Galleries of Scotland photography collection. Louise has previously held positions at the Smithsonian, the Royal Collection Trust, and the National Library of Scotland.

Karine Polwart, BBC Radio 2 Folk Singer of the Year 2018, is a multi-award-winning Scottish songwriter and musician, as well as theatre-maker, storyteller, spoken-word performer, and author. Her songs combine folk influences and myth with themes as diverse as Donald Trump's corporate megalomania, Charles Darwin's family life, and the complexities of modern parenthood. She sings traditional songs, too, and writes for film, theatre, animation, and thematic collaborative projects. Karine is a seven-time winner at the BBC Radio 2 Folk Awards, including three wins for Best Original Song.

www.karinepolwart.com

Lesley Riddoch is an award-winning broadcaster, journalist, author, cyclist, and land-reform campaigner. She is one of Scotland's best-known commentators and broadcasters. Lesley went to Oxford University (where she was the first non-Tory president of the Student's Union) and did a post-graduate course at Cardiff University. She is best known for broadcasting with programmes on BBC2, Channel 4, Radio 4, and BBC Radio Scotland, for which she won two Sony speech broadcaster awards. Lesley is a weekly columnist for the *Scotsman* and the *National* and a regular contributor to the *Guardian*, *Scotland Tonight*, *BBC Question Time*, and *Any Question*s.

www.lesleyriddoch.com

PERMISSIONS

Best efforts have been made by the author to gain permissions from all persons and publications for works reproduced in the book. Thank you to the following institutions, collections, and individuals for allowing reproduction including licencing, for the purpose of this publication. All images of and quotes from the Menie residents have been shared with permission to Alicia Bruce.

P. 10
Patricia and Angus Macdonald, from the *Playgrounds* series: *bunkered terrain, Menie, and Trump International Golf Links on the remains of the dunes at Menie; 2015.* (2015) Reproduced with kind permission from Patricia and Angus Macdonald.

P. 11
The original Trump International Golf Links Scotland developers' map, designed by golf architects Hawtree Ltd.

P. 88
Erik Hoffmann, *Nightfall: Portrait of George Mackay Brown* (1988)
© Aberdeen City Council (Archives, Gallery & Museums Collection).
Reproduced with kind permission from Erik Hoffman.

P. 88
Archibald D. Reid, *On the Bents* (1873)
© Aberdeen City Council (Archives, Gallery & Museums Collection).

P. 89
James Guthrie, *To Pastures New* (1883)
© Aberdeen City Council (Archives, Gallery & Museums Collection).

P. 89 & P. 107
Grant Wood, *American Gothic* (1930)
Friends of American Art Collection, Art Institute of Chicago.

P. 90
Thomas Faed, *The Reaper* (1863)
© Aberdeen City Council (Archives, Gallery & Museums Collection).

P. 90
Arthur Hughes, *The Mower* (1865)
© Aberdeen City Council (Archives, Gallery & Museums Collection).

P. 91
Victoria Crowe, *Large Tree Group* (1975)
National Galleries of Scotland. Presented by Mr and Mrs John Butters through the Patrons of the National Galleries of Scotland 2015.
© Victoria Crowe. With special thanks to Victoria Crowe and Gemma Gray.

P. 92
Sir James Guthrie, *A Hind's Daughter* (1883)
National Galleries of Scotland. Bequest of Sir James Lewis Caw 1951.

P. 92
Auguste Renoir, *Dance in the Country* or *Danse à la campagne* (1883)
© RMN (Musée d'Orsay).

P. 93
Jules Breton, *The Gleaner* (1875)
© Aberdeen City Council (Archives, Gallery & Museums Collection).

P. 93
Joan Eardley RSA, *Salmon Nets on the Shore* (1961)
© The Eardley Estate. With special thanks to Anne Eardley.

P. 106
D.O. Hill RSA, *The First General Assembly of the Free Church of Scotland; signing the Act of Separation and Deed of Demission – 18th May 1843* (1843)
Image © Free Church of Scotland.
Reproduced with the kind permission of the Free Church of Scotland.

P. 107
David Octavius Hill and Robert Adamson, *Jeanie Wilson [Newhaven 15]* (1843–1857)
National Galleries of Scotland.

P. 107
Milton Rogovin, *Family of Miners (1981–1990) Scotland*
National Galleries of Scotland. Gift of David Knaus, 2018.
Collection Center for Creative Photography.
© Rogovin Collection.

TIMELINE

A contribution of research for this timeline includes, but is not limited to:

Alicia Bruce's personal archive.

David and Moira Milne's personal archive, reproduced with kind permission of David and Moira Milne.

Andy Wightman's report 'Donald Trump's Ego Trip', 2011, reproduced with kind permission of Andy Wightman.

P. T1
Belhelvie Jubilee Gazette, (1935)
Scotland's Moving Image Archive.

P. T2
The original Trump International Golf Links Scotland developers' map, designed by golf architects Hawtree Ltd. Collection of Debra Storr and Aberdeenshire Council.

P. T3
Approved Trump International Golf Links Scotland master plan, Gareth Hoskins Architects.

P. T6
Detail: Approved Trump International Golf Links Scotland master plan, Gareth Hoskins Architects.

P. T10
Susan Munro, Anthony Baxter, and Alicia Bruce at premiere of *You've Been Trumped* (2011)
Photograph by Rohan Beyts, reproduced

with kind permission of the photographer. Poster artwork (2010) reproduced with kind permission of David McCue, artist, and Montrose Pictures

P. T14
21 January 2017 Women's March in Edinburgh.
Photograph by Andrew Rafferty.

Timeline Tip Ins

Tip In #1
Trump's 'Personal Invitation' to Menie residents. Source: David and Moira Milne's personal archive. Reproduced with kind permission of David and Moira Milne.

Tip In #2
Letter from David Kennedy to Professor John Harper renouncing his honorary degree previously conferred upon him. Reproduced with kind permission of David Kennedy.

Tip In #3
Letter from Donald Trump to First Minister Alex Salmond. Source: Andy Wightman's report 'Donald Trump's Ego Trip', 2011. Reproduced with permission of Andy Wightman.

Tip In #4
Article 'Top Scot Forbes makes a spirited return', *The Scotsman*, 1 December 2012,

P.16–17.
Reproduced with permission of Brian Ferguson, journalist, and Phil Wilkinson, photographer.

Tip In #5
Obituary, Molly Forbes, *The Scotsman*, 10 May 2021, P. 37.
Reproduced with permission of Susan Mansfield, Art Critic, *The Scotsman*.

Other cited works from:

Aberdeen Journals Ltd
Aberdeenshire Council Planning and
    Environmental Services
BBC News
BBC Panorama's *The Trouble with Trump*
Donald Trump
Dundas and Wilson
DC Thompson
Gareth Hoskins Architects
Grampian Police
Prof Jim Hansom, School of
    Geographical and Earth Sciences
Karine Polwart & Steven Polwart
Montrose Pictures
The Munro Family
STV News
The Aberdonian
The Daily Mail
Tripping Up Trump
University of Glasgow

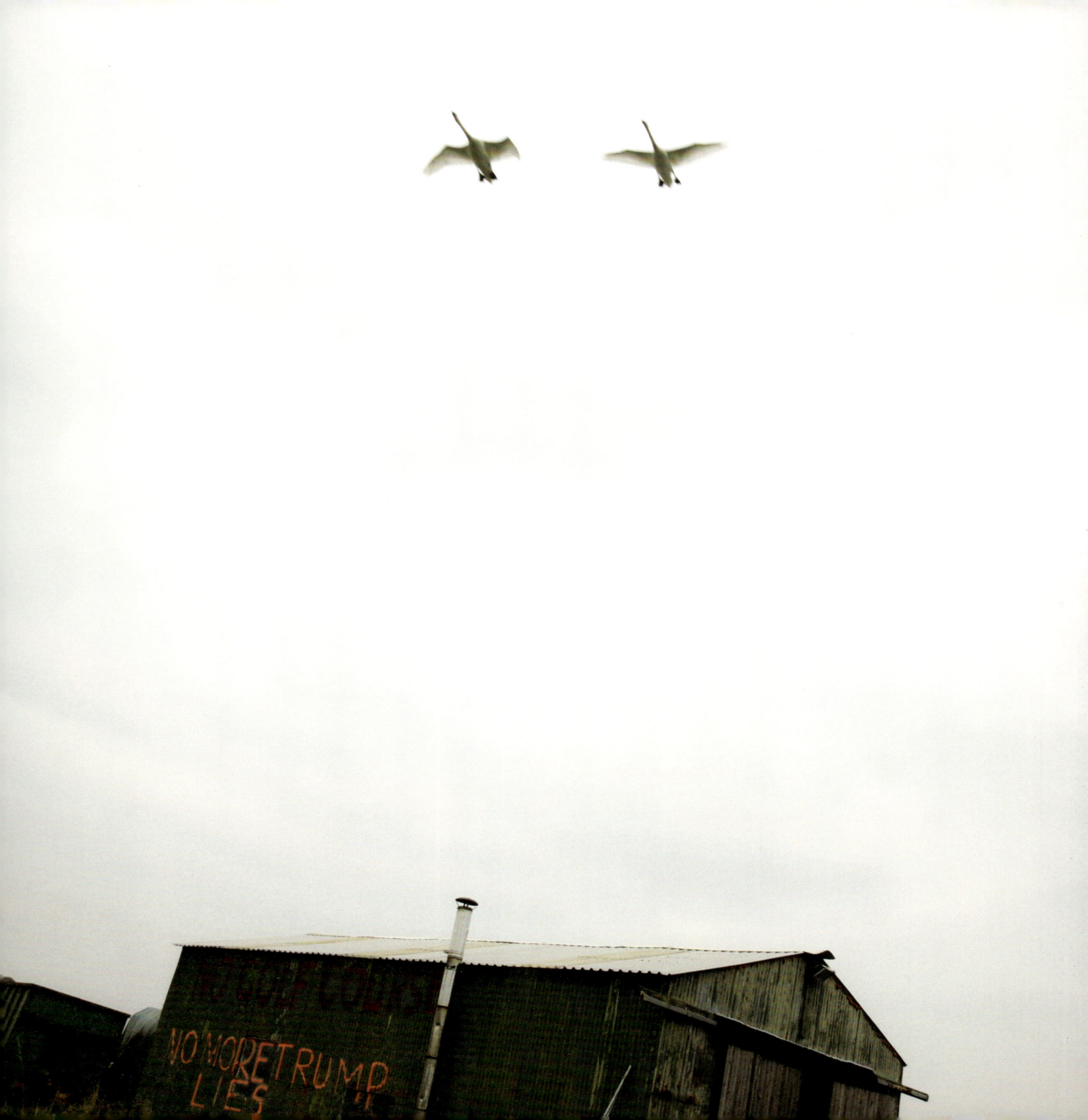